Boyle County Public Library

WILL PRYCE

BIG SHED

240 illustrations, 228 in color

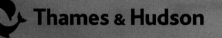
Thames & Hudson

For Elvis

P. 1 Inchon Transportation Centre, Inchon Airport,
      South Korea (Terry Farrell & Partners)

PP. 2–3 Zenith, Rouen (Bernard Tschumi)

First published in 2007 in hardcover in the United States of America by
Thames & Hudson Inc., 500 Fifth Avenue, New York, New York 10110

thamesandhudsonusa.com

Library of Congress Catalog Card Number: 2006908829

ISBN-13: 978-0-500-34234-3

Printed and bound in Singapore by CS Graphics

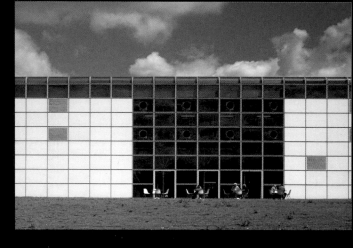

Exhibition

Industry

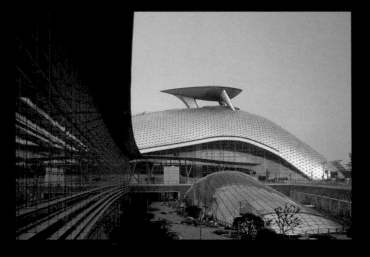

Transport

Sport

Arts

Influence

PREFACE

To set foot in the departure lounge of Kansai Airport for the first time can be a humbling experience. This extraordinary one-and-a-half kilometre (one mile) long tube gently curves in three dimensions, its steel ribs, woven like a wicker basket, stretching out above our heads into the distance. At first this enormous room seems reminiscent only of science fiction, yet there is also something about it that is quite familiar. We can recall searching for frozen peas among the endless featureless aisles of a provincial superstore, playing five-a-side football under yellowish light in an echoing sports centre, and being jostled in the dark recesses of a vast warehouse by a frantic crowd in search of cut-price Scandinavian furniture. Unlike the grandeur of Kansai these memories are of buildings that aren't credited with the title of 'architecture' at all. Instead they are usually described as 'sheds' – or, as they are often of a considerable size, 'big sheds'. But what does this choice of vocabulary entail?

'Shed' tends to describe a building whose purpose is not apparent from the outside, and which consists of simple diagrammatic spaces rather than functionally determined rooms. A 'shed', unlike a 'building', warrants no assumption of permanence, and is viewed as having a specific, and comparatively short, lifespan. These simple boxes litter the outskirts of our towns and cities and service the space-hungry low-cost functions with which we have become familiar. During the past twenty years both the number and size of these structures has risen greatly.[1] At the time of writing a proposal for the largest building in Europe is planned for a site at Pyrstock, in England. Described in the press as 'The Megashed' it is designed to service a supermarket chain and will have a floorspace of 116,125 square metres (1.25 million square feet), larger than London's Millennium Dome.

But our own experience tells us that sports centres and warehouses built cheaply on the outskirts of cities are not the only structures that have these characteristics. If we use the same criteria to judge many high-profile buildings by famous architects we find that they also have shed-like features. They are massive and ground-hugging, and often contain a cavernous single space. It is often impossible to judge from the exterior of the building which sections contain which activities, and is much easier to discern the individual structural modules than to determine what those modules contain. Moreover, they are primarily constructed using steel frames, which have the structural capacity to span great distances using comparatively slim members. They also enclose a large area for the weight of their structures, and in this sense sheds are 'lightweight' buildings.

The architectural writer Hugh Pearman recognized that, 'at a casual glance' airports seem to be 'simply great big sheds.'[2] Yet he went on to explain that they are in fact complex buildings, 'part transport interchange, part factory, part distribution centre, part shopping mall'.[3] Simply because we can comprehend their great programmatic complexity, however, doesn't rid these structures of their 'shed-like' character. Kansai Airport can have a very complex function, be an architectural masterpiece and still intelligently be described as a 'shed'. And it is a shed not simply because it reminds us of the sheds with which we are familiar but because it is the product of a distinct and coherent school of thought that consciously determined its shed-like characteristics. To describe it as a 'shed' is not therefore a semantic quibble but an accurate definition of this type of structure. And these structures are now so influential that their use goes far beyond airports or factories: indeed their influence can be seen in important civic buildings such as libraries and arts centres, typologies that traditionally defined what 'architecture' was understood to be.

As ever, theories of design have been tempered by practicalities and the rise of the big shed, like the skyscraper before it, is as much a consequence of economics as aesthetics. This book asks how this phenomenon has come about and what it can tell us about contemporary architecture.

ORIGINS

ORIGINS
Problem-solvers and Shapemakers

In 1994 Norman Foster delivered a lecture at Hong Kong University. Describing his new airport at Stansted he talked almost entirely about the building's cheapness and efficiency. At the end of the lecture a student asked why Foster had talked so much about economics and so little about aesthetics – to which Foster replied that if the student did not understand that he *had* been talking about aesthetics then there was nothing more to be said. The origins of the shed lie at the source of this confusion. For the design of large-span and large-volume buildings like Stansted, quite apart from being an exercise in logistics and engineering, involves the conscious application of an aesthetic principle, in this case one assumed by Foster but not by the student.

Historically, an architectural style established that a building's appearance would be determined not solely by its practical requirements, but also by the use of a recognized visual grammar of motifs. However complex the building's structure, the final architectural formulation also required the application of an aesthetic system. Technical innovation was not considered a prerequisite of great architecture. Sometimes the most influential buildings, such as the Pantheon or Hagia Sophia, were structurally innovative; sometimes, like Blenheim Palace or Versailles, they were not.

Since the advent of the Modern Movement at the beginning of the 20th century, however,

technical sophistication has played a much greater role in how a building is judged. The first apologists for the new approach were the art historians Sigfried Giedion and Nikolaus Pevsner. In their view, the 19th-century architectural profession had blundered into a terrible cultural cul-de-sac by reviving the classical and gothic styles. But an alternative was to be found in the technical achievements of a group of 19th-century designers. These men had satisfied the needs of the industrial revolution by building bridges, exhibition halls and train termini. Because these were engineers designing with iron, rather than architects building in monumental masonry, the architectural profession considered their products outside the realms of its subject. The views of the German architect Jakob Wolf lecturing in 1846 were typical: 'iron may be used, where it is intended for temporary use. Monumental architecture, conceived for eternal life, must be reserved for masonry.'[1] John Ruskin, writing in *The Seven Lamps of Architecture* (1849), agreed that 'true architecture does not admit iron as a constructive material, and that...the iron roofs and pillars of our railway stations...are not architecture at all.'[2]

Giedion and Pevsner believed that these engineers were, on the contrary, pioneering a new architecture based explicitly upon technical innovation. As Giedion declared in *Space, Time and Architecture* (1941): 'the seeds of the architecture of our day were to be found in

technical developments.'[3] They were not suggesting, however, that 19th-century engineers were themselves mature architects. On the contrary, Giedion quoted the Art Nouveau architect Henry van de Velde, who suggested that: 'The extraordinary beauty innate in the work of engineers has its basis in their unconsciousness of its artistic possibilities.'[4] According to Giedion, it was only with the first generation of 'modern' architects, such as Peter Behrens and Walter Gropius, that the technical achievements of the 'noble savages' of the 19th century were harnessed to an aesthetic end – the creation of the Modern Movement.

Pevsner included an even more extensive survey of the achievements of the 19th-century engineers in his book, *Pioneers of the Modern Movement* (1936). Like Giedion, Pevsner's enthusiasm was based on his firm belief, derived from the philosopher Hegel, in the existence of a *zeitgeist*, a 'spirit of the age', which determined the particular course architecture should take. Pevsner justified his favourite buildings by discerning the origins of the zeitgeist in the work of their architects. It was architects such as Gropius, particularly in his Fagus Works of 1911, who provided 'the fulfilment of the style of our century; entirely representative of the spirit of today'.[5]

Pevsner then demanded that other practitioners of the Modern Movement utilize the template these men had provided. Architects who built instead in an expressionistic

PREVIOUS SPREAD West façade, Sainsbury Centre

FOLLOWING SPREAD The Pompidou Centre's iconic external
servicing was pushed to the periphery only
in order to leave a neutral volume inside.

form of modernism, for example, were criticized
for failing to take their responsibilities to the
zeitgeist seriously enough. Consequently they
were excluded from his description of the
history of the movement. Their chief sin was to
give their buildings a recognizable personal
form.[6] Pevsner viewed Expressionism, along
with the work of Gaudí, the Brazilian modernists
and 'all those who imitate them', as, 'attempts
to satisfy the craving of architects for individual
expression…and for an escape out of reality
into a fairy world'.[7] When he re-released his
book as Pioneers of Modern Design in 1960,
Pevsner went on to explain clearly that the
architectural style of the Modern Movement
had been created at one point in time and the
responsibility now was to follow the early
masters such as Gropius, Le Corbusier and
Mies van de Rohe.[8]

This view, that the large-span and large-
volume buildings of the 19th century were
merely detached forerunners of the early
modernists, remained unchallenged until the
1950s. Curiously, when the critique came it
was delivered with the same unshakeable faith
in the inevitable existence of a Modern
Movement, though one whose purity had been
sullied by Pevsner's conceptual errors. The art
historian Reyner Banham had been a pupil of
Pevsner's at the Courtauld Institute in London.
But in an essay published in a book honouring
Pevsner, Concerning Architecture (1968)
Banham complained that, 'those of my

generation who interrupted their architectural
training in order to fight a war to make the
world safe for the Modern Movement',[9] had
been betrayed by Pevsner's acceptance of the
possibility of regional architectural styles.
For Banham, saving the world from Hitler
was merely a convenient by-product of
implementing the new architecture.

Banham presented his views in his book,
Theory and Design in the First Machine Age
(1960). Just as Pevsner believed that some
architects were working within the zeitgeist,
Banham accepted that 'each age has legitimate
and authentic forms of expression.'[10] However,
Banham maintained that if the Modern
Movement had been the product of a particular
current of technological innovation then,
logically, it would have to follow technology
wherever that might lead. Science might
ultimately pursue a path that would change the
way 'modernism' was understood. Banham
went on to suggest that the first generation of
Modern Movement architects were not as
machine age as they might first appear. In many
ways the work of the 19th-century engineers
involved a much more honest expression of the
latest technology. The 'machine aesthetic' was,
by and large, just that: an aesthetic.

Banham began his critique by taking
Le Corbusier's famous juxtaposition of
automobiles and the Parthenon. He noted that
the automobiles chosen were not mass-
produced but were 'expensive, specialized,

handicraft one-offs which can justly be
compared to the Parthenon because, like it,
they are unique works of handmade art.'[11]
He went on to point out that while vehicles and
ships initially favoured the simple strong forms
beloved of the modernists, they then developed
very different designs wholly unlike
International Style buildings. For car and
ship designers were not trying to perfect an
appearance but instead were trying to solve a
group of completely different problems: 'the
order which Le Corbusier had to offer proved
finally, in spite of all the carryings-on about the
motorcar, etcetera, to be the pre-technological
order of the peasant economy.'[12] For Banham,
Le Corbusier's buildings were sculptural, highly
individual, and did not lend themselves to
mass production.

Banham's critique exposed a key
distinction between the modernists and the
19th-century engineers. The modernists viewed
architecture as a social and political force, one
that could actively improve society, whereas
the engineers had more limited ambitions.
Central to Le Corbusier's philosophy, for
example, was a faith in the importance of
planning, whereby an individual architect could
determine all of the spaces and therefore all of
the functions of the building himself. For Le
Corbusier the art of architecture had a political
dimension: by controlling the size and
arrangement of internal volumes you could
control the building's function and, to some

extent, what went on in it. When Le Corbusier proclaimed, 'the plan is the generator' he was recognizing the means by which the architect could determine the building's contents, which for him was the essence of design. Concrete, being very malleable, enabled him simply to extrude these decisions into a finished building. At the same time concrete also provided the smooth finishes and simple volumes that suited his formal visual concerns. For Joseph Paxton, the designer of the Crystal Palace and Isambard Kingdom Brunel, the designer of Paddington Station, their remit only included the provision of a neutral volume whose contents would be determined by someone else.

Banham also recognized that the early modernists, like the architects of the Beaux-Arts before them, were still concerned with the provision of a recognizable architectural language. While less critical of Mies van de Rohe than Le Corbusier, Banham viewed Mies's fascination with beautiful details as ultimately indicative of a craft mentality. Ultimately Mies's determination to clad the concrete-covered steel of his Seagram Building with external steel I-beams proved that it was more important to him that the steel structure was visually legible than that it was an efficient use of technology.

Banham's view – that the profession had misunderstood the relationship between architecture and technology – reflected the changes he had witnessed taking place in society since the Second World War. The war had

been a catalyst, encouraging fresh technological solutions to architectural problems, which in its aftermath were given immediate impetus by the need to alleviate a housing crisis. This appeared to offer an opportunity for architects to customize the production lines that had served the war effort in order to build houses. However, as Colin Davies has described in his book *The Prefabricated Home*, while prefabricated houses have had a successful history, the involvement of a famous architect has always been disastrous. After the war several attempts were made to produce lightweight housing using redundant aircraft factories. Jean Prouvé designed a version in France, while the British Aeroplane Company produced 54,000 AIROH (Aircraft Industry Research Organization on Housing) houses. But certainly the most radical (and arguably ultimately the least successful) attempt to mass-produce houses, was that of the inventor Richard Buckminster Fuller in the United States.

Fuller developed the prototype 'Wichita House' of 1944 in conjunction with the Beech Aircraft Corporation of Wichita, Kansas. The house provided over 93 square metres (1,000 square feet) of centrally heated floorspace, while weighing less than 3,500 kilogrammes (7,700 pounds). Whether Fuller had become an obsessive perfectionist or whether he recognized some hitherto unforeseen technical problem, he refused to let the house go into production, citing the need for further development, and

only one house was ever built. But Banham saw in Fuller an alternative understanding of architecture's relationship with technology. Banham's enthusiasm would ultimately make a powerful impression on a young generation of architects. Central to Fuller's appeal was his radical interpretation of what 'architecture' was.

Throughout his life Fuller remained outside conventional architectural circles. He was a man with profoundly serious views about technology that had been developed after a personal crisis in a manner that resembled a religious conversion. The death of his daughter and loss of his job resulted in Fuller's 'year of silence' during which he did not talk to anyone (including his wife) but read furiously and formulated a series of highly original proposals for prefabricated structures. After their failure, and an unsuccessful attempt to mass-produce a new type of car, Fuller finally found widespread international recognition for his geodesic dome. All of his ideas were based upon an adamant belief in the process of continuous technological evolution, which he described as the 'unhaltable trend to constantly accelerating change.'[13] Fuller believed that new technologies would offer alternative solutions to conventional architectural problems, his famous dictum being that: 'the answer to the housing problem lies on the way to the moon.'[14] As a consequence, all of Fuller's prefabricated houses were designed as part of a broader idea about weight and efficiency. They were simply part of his plan for a new mass-produced human-life-protecting service industry.

At the time, Fuller's ideas were either ignored or denigrated by the majority of the architectural profession. His work provoked hostility because it undermined the cultural significance of architecture through its insistence on perpetual change. With his idea of 'ephemeralization', Fuller believed that because of continuous technical innovation all architectural achievements must ultimately have a shelf life as better solutions are invented. He accepted that his own designs would shortly be rendered obsolete, but then so would everyone else's. At best his prefabricated solutions were viewed as being outside the remit of architects, who were still fundamentally interested in the erection of permanent structures. As architect Philip Johnson wrote in 1960, 'Let Bucky Fuller put together the Dymaxion dwellings of the people so long as we architects can design their tombs and monuments.'[15] When Fuller offered the drawings of his original prefabricated Dymaxion House (1927) to the American Institute of Architects they were returned.

Fuller questioned the purpose of architectural design. Seeing any problem within the context of 'the bigger picture' he proposed that issues traditionally addressed by spatial ingenuity, such as making certain rooms face south, could actually be solved by a technical gadget. Fuller also further formalized the idea of 'technology transfer', the principle pioneered by Paxton, whereby the products of one industry could be used to innovate in another. As a consequence the manufacturing expertise for the Wichita House was provided not by the housing industry, but by the Butler Company of Kansas, a firm that built metal grain silos.

At the beginning of the 1960s a number of architects began to follow the precepts of Fuller by exploring, at least on paper, the potential for technology to transform architectural design. At the World Design Conference of 1960 in Tokyo a group of young Japanese architects declared themselves 'Metabolists', with a series of paper projects that proposed a new biological model for architecture. The following year in London, another group of young architects working for large practices entertained themselves by publishing a magazine called *Archigram*. And in July of that year two architecture students, Richard Rogers and Norman Foster, struck up a conversation at a reception for students commencing their masters degrees at Yale.

The Metabolists group had been formed in a deliberate attempt to replicate the self-publicizing tactics of European and American designers. They were interested in designing buildings that allowed for future alteration in the same way that organisms changed and adapted in the natural world. In most of their schemes this resulted in the basic idea that there could be a permanent servicing armature onto which temporary capsules could be added or removed. By the mid-1960s they had at least encouraged an aesthetic in Japanese architecture that suggested incompleteness. In Kenzo Tange's 'Yamanashi Press and Broadcasting Centre' (1961–7), for example, the primary structural elements were circular service shafts, from which large horizontal beams were cantilevered to support the offices and studios. Some gaps were deliberately left on the cylinders to suggest that further platforms could be added at a later date. However, the whole was built permanently in concrete, looking rather like an oil-rig that had been turned to stone.

The Osaka Expo in 1970, the first major World's Fair to be held in Asia, provided the first real opportunity to build some of these Metabolist ideas. The Expo was an enormous success with 64 million people attending the fair in its first six months. Kenzo Tange's Festival Plaza, Kiyonori Kikutake's 125-metre (410-foot) Expo Tower and Kisho Kurokawa's Takara Pavilion all suggested Metabolist themes. After the Expo, Kurokawa used pod construction in a commercial scheme, the Nakagin Tower (1972), which was designed to provide a block of mid-week boltholes for overworked Tokyo commuters. All the apartments were essentially single-room dwellings, 4 by 2.5 metres (13 by 8 feet), made from shipping containers that had been craned into position on a serviced structural armature. All their amenities were miniaturized and built-in except a stove –

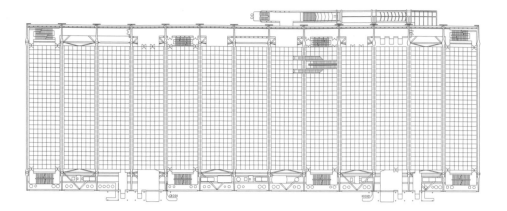

since the building was located in the restaurant district its occupants were expected to eat out.

In Britain, meanwhile, the architects' collective Archigram similarly proposed a new role for architecture based upon its relationship with technology. Frustrated by tedious jobs in conventional practices, the founders of Archigram started out as a loose collection of architects who met up after work. A group of six – Warren Chalk, Peter Cook, Dennis Crompton, David Greene, Ron Herron and Mike Webb – became permanent members of the architectural think-tank. Archigram formulated a set of fantasy architecture proposals, which they then published between 1961 and 1974 in nine editions of a magazine of the same name.

The Metabolists and Archigram were not the first architectural groups to challenge the prevailing orthodoxy of the Modern Movement, whose official position was expressed by the Congrès Internationaux d'Architecture Moderne (CIAM). During the early 1960s the revisionist group Team X had built a series of projects that Banham was to describe as 'the new Brutalism'.[16] These 'Brutalists' took the very basic 19th-century technology that lay at the heart of the post-war building industry, including reinforced concrete poured on site, plate glass and brickwork, and fetishized its 'wet construction' credentials and low technology origins. Two Archigram members, Ron Herron and Warren Chalk, actually worked on one of the icons of the new style, the South Bank Centre in

London (1960–64). Once Brutalism was in full swing, however, the visionary work of Archigram explored the opposite approach based on factory production.

In many ways the group's work reflected a more general national sense of optimism that resulted from the availability of new goods and services. During the 1950s many Europeans had access to indoor toilets for the first time, swiftly followed by washing machines and motorcars, which in 1957 had led Prime Minister Harold Macmillan famously to claim that most Britons had 'never had it so good'.[17] As technological optimists, the Archigram group took these practical innovations to their logical conclusion in a series of hypothetical projects. Inspired by the partial success of the Metabolists, they reasoned that if domestic products can be plumbed in to the house, could the house not be plumbed in and clipped on to the city, as Peter Cook's 'Plug-in City' scheme of 1964 suggested?

Like Buckminster Fuller, members of Archigram believed that during a period of continuous technical innovation any building would, necessarily, date very quickly. As a consequence they proposed buildings that were assembled ad hoc or were incomplete and therefore capable of further adjustment. They refused to accept the central principle of their profession, that architects could offer a complete solution to their clients' requirements. Instead they proposed an approximate solution, with buildings capable of future manipulation by

their inhabitants. As their magazine suggested in 1966, 'buildings with no capacity to change can only become slums or ancient monuments.'[18]

One of *Archigram* magazine's occasional contributors was Cedric Price, an unashamed iconoclast and provocateur who managed to remain an 'enfant terrible' throughout his career. He professed, for example, a belief that England's cathedrals should be pulled down because they had been around too long and asked why the stones of Stonehenge couldn't be re-used. However facetious his examples Price sincerely questioned a central tenant of architectural thinking – that buildings were permanent. Price even fought for years to get one of his own buildings demolished. His most influential project – The Fun Palace (1965) – was designed for Joan Littlewood's theatre. It proposed a single permanent structure that acted as an armature for a whole series of flexible and changeable elements. Price encouraged people to think of a brief in wholly diagrammatic terms as a problem whose solution might or might not be conventionally architectural. He is reputed to have gone to a client meeting with a married couple in order to discuss the design for their house and concluded the meeting by recommending that the couple divorce.

The ideas of Archigram and Cedric Price, while highly influential, remained largely unbuilt and unbuildable. Instead their importance lies in the impact these ideas had on architects

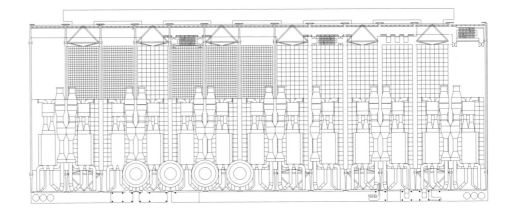

educated in the 1960s. During the following decade two of the most prominent of them, Richard Rogers and Norman Foster, went on to erect buildings that gave an original form to ideas latent in these separate influences. In turn their buildings would affect the priorities and views of many other architects.

At Yale Rogers and Foster had been taught by a Russian émigré called Serge Chermayeff, then in the process of writing a book with Christopher Alexander, which became *Community and Privacy* (1963). Chermayeff was not interested in modernism as a formal code, but as a means to organize the relationship between the character of spaces, the balance between public and private areas of the city. He believed that the appearance of a building did not affect its success or failure. Looking at contemporary architects he made his preferences clear: 'I hope that our shapemakers will, like old soldiers, or the Cheshire Cat, fade away with their "creations". I hope to see them replaced by "problem-solvers".'[19] To be a 'shapemaker' was to approach the issue of architectural design as an issue of finding an appropriate visual form. To be a 'problem-solver' was to recognize the essential practical issues that concern the scheme and then to use diagrams to delineate a strategic response. The final appearance of the building would simply reflect the diagrammatic solution. The question, in other words, was whether a building would 'work', its appearance being simply a by-

product of its conception. As Richard Rogers recalled in 2000 'We believed everything he said. His concise intellectual framework is still with us.'[20]

Rogers and Foster also travelled to the West Coast of the United States where they were inspired by one of the most iconic (if equally unsuccessful) attempts of recognized architects to encourage the prefabrication of modernist houses. The Case Study Houses, particularly those by Craig Ellwood, Pierre Koenig and Raphael Soriano, were single-storey open-planned structures framed in timber or steel. Designed as exemplars, they had the appearance of universal designs that could be replicated and erected anywhere. Case Study House 8 (built 1945–9), designed by Charles Eames and his wife Ray for their own use, went one step further, utilizing standard off-the-peg steel and glass components. While none of these houses became mass-produced, they had a mass-production aesthetic. Indeed, Colin Davies neatly summarizes them as examples of the 'one-off mass-produced house' that appealed to Rogers and Foster. Henceforth both architects would seek to distance the process of construction as much as possible from site. Choosing lightweight and prefabricated materials they developed modular systems that at least had the appearance of mass-produced kits-of-parts.

In 1970 Richard Rogers formed a partnership with the Italian architect Renzo

Piano, and the following year they won a competition for the **Pompidou Centre** in Paris. The brainchild of the then French President Georges Pompidou, this complex for the contemporary arts was to be built on a 3-hectare (7.5-acre) site in the centre of Paris, which had been cleared in the 1930s and was serving as a car park for trucks supplying the nearby market at Les Halles.

Piano and Rogers designed the scheme using simple diagrams. The upper limit of the building zone was controlled by Parisian fire regulations that determined that no building could be higher than a fireman's hose. A basic oblong became the form of the scheme, and, despite a brief post-competition flirtation with other shapes, the Pompidou would remain rectilinear. Within this essential 'container' form they decided to provide a totally flexible interior, which resulted in a completely clear cross-span. Consequently all the servicing was pushed to one side of the scheme, all the public access areas to the other side. To span the intervening 45 metres (150 feet) demanded very strong trusses. These presented a difficulty in that they would have to be very deep and would detract from the now precious height.

The solution was to adopt a double-layered external steel skeleton. Here the columns of the inner layer worked in compression, the thin outer layer in tension with a type of cantilever beam, a 'gerberette', transferring the load in between. Named after

their inventor, a 19th-century German engineer called Heinrich Gerber, these were used at the suggestion of structural engineer Peter Rice. They were made of cast steel following the practice Rice had witnessed being used by architect Kenzo Tange in Japan. The subtlety of the whole system lies in linking the truss girder, column and tie without putting additional localized 'eccentric' loads on the column. To achieve this the gerberette has spherical bearings that allow it to flex and rotate without transferring these loads to the column. The result is a structure made up of eleven internal steel frames and two end-braced gable frames – thus thirteen bays in all. The bays are 12.8 metres (42 feet) wide giving the building an overall length of 166.4 metres (545 feet). At 42 metres (138 feet) high and 60 metres (197 feet) wide, it contains a volume of 430,000 cubic metres (over 15 million cubic feet).

The Pompidou Centre opened in January 1977. Piano remarked that the only logical improvement they could have made to this building, conceived as a neutral volume, would have been the removal of the interior to leave an empty skeleton. This 'shed-like' quality was at the heart of its critical reception. Archigram's Peter Cook declared that 'its where it's at… a well equipped hangar.' But Alan Colquhoun, writing in *Architectural Design*, launched a withering attack on its shed-like form. Piano and Rogers' scheme had been unique among the competition entries in ignoring the existing urban fabric, the architectural axes and public arcades, rooflines and forms. According to Colquhoun this resulted in a scheme of brilliant simplicity and clarity, 'in which the entire building was flexible and…consisted of a series of superimposed and uniform loft spaces'.[21] These innovations, however, were precisely the reasons why Colquhoun went on to criticize the scheme so thoroughly. He felt that the result of this audaciously simple solution was 'a vast self-sufficient block, inserted rather crudely into the city fabric.' Colquhoun asked difficult questions, such as what possible function requires a clear 50-metre (164-foot) span within a 7-metre (23-foot) height limit, of which 3 metres (10 feet) is filled with lattice beams? Originally the removal of all columns was related to a competition idea of adjustable floor-heights but once this idea was dropped the spaces left felt compressed with low ceiling heights for their size. The core of Colquhoun's attack was the fact that the entire design resulted from two fundamental decisions: 'that the building should be conceived of as a well-serviced shed and that its symbolism should be concerned with its mechanical support systems.'

Undeniably, the design of the building focused on providing a clear span to a degree which was no longer simply practical but ideological. Just one set of internal columns would have halved the depth of the truss girders and possibly done the same to the cost of the building. As Renzo Piano commented afterwards 'Once you put the column in the centre, it doesn't only mean to put the column. Then it becomes perfectly logical to put one lift and maybe some pipes…in a sense, our building's quality, its value, is in its extremity.'[22] Both critic and architect fundamentally agreed on how the building had been conceived, just not the desirability of such a choice. Indeed, it was the same quality of conceptual radicalism centred on this very simple diagram that also galvanized the building's supporters. Hilton Kramer, writing in *The New York Times* declared that the Pompidou 'is one of the most breathtaking architectural accomplishments of recent times, and certainly the most radical modernist building ever to be erected in Paris'.[23] That radicalism was perceived to be of two distinct kinds: first its obvious and very simple large-span diagram, and second the engineering marshalled to resolve that diagram. As Mark Stevens wrote in *Newsweek*: 'The building celebrates…process over form and declares that technology – as symbolized by the architecture – may be a toy for casual pleasure.'[24]

The Pompidou Centre became a hugely popular icon because of its shed-like form. Its hugeness, blockiness and insensitivity to its surrounding buildings became a unique draw in such a homogenous historic area of the city. Six million people visited the centre in its first year, making it easily the most popular attraction in Paris. It still receives in excess of six million visitors a year. And this reveals one of the

OPPOSITE Not actually a solid frame, the Sainsbury
Centre was designed with three
prismatic trusses creating a kind of
'post and beam' structure.

FOLLOWING SPREAD The neutral volume of the Sainsbury
Centre – all its functions fit within an
independent envelope.

fundamental facts about this building: its context. Its radicalism is amplified by its juxtaposition with the 19th-century Parisian cityscape. The Lloyds Building in London, by comparison, is in a more heterogeneous context and becomes less of a remarkable oddity as further new buildings surround it. The precious location of the Pompidou in a zone of conserved historic city maintains its shock value.

Norman Foster's **Sainsbury Centre for Visual Arts** opened the following year. Like the Pompidou this building turned the typology of 'arts centre' on its head. Foster was simply not interested in the traditional approach to designing a building with this type of brief. While most architects would begin by determining the constituent rooms in the building and planning their relationship, Foster Associates' strategy was diagrammatic, tackling the problem from first principles. They chose a system of construction that would enclose a large neutral space, which could then be split up using temporary partitions. Even the second storey would sit as a mezzanine under an oversailing roof. The result is a building that closely resembles a rigid welded portal frame, a building system that had become very popular after the war. It is not actually a portal frame but uses prismatic trusses to create a kind of 'post and beam' system. One horizontal truss makes up the beam, which is then pin-and-slip jointed to the vertical trusses making up the 'posts'. This was not only a technical development

on the solid portal frame used at the Team 4 factory building for Reliance Controls but an extraordinary choice for a major arts commission. It created a huge extruded shape containing a single volume 120 metres (394 feet) long, 75 metres (250 feet) wide and 35 metres (115 feet) high, within which all the various functions of the centre were located.

The building's structure contains within its depth a service zone that housed the WCs, stores and kitchen areas. This allows for the continuous surfaces of both interior and exterior walls and accommodated gantries in the roof so that services could be maintained without entering the gallery space. The inner skin is composed of fixed louvres laid horizontally. The wrap-around outer cladding was developed in collaboration with industrial designer Tony Prichard. It is comprised of 1.8- by 1.2-metre (6- by 4-foot) sandwich panels. These contain a thin layer of anodized aluminium behind which lies a deep layer of insulating phenolic foam sealed up with a neoprene gasket lattice. Originally described as 'super-plastic' aluminium, the cladding panels were moulded like plastic and then fastened onto the structure with six bolts. The advantage of this system is that panels can be moved in just a few minutes. Their silvery colour was designed to reflect the radiant heat of the sun. The same cladding was chosen for the roof and the walls. Foster Associates explained this was because the roof would serve as a 'fifth façade' as it was overlooked by

the buildings of the original campus. But the creation of an even simpler and more consistent diagram must have provided the real satisfaction.

The Sainsbury Centre was a clear statement of intent from Foster that any commission – even an art gallery – would be treated in the same diagrammatic way. The architect Leon Krier felt that looking at the building he was 'in the presence of an extremely stubborn man, who, given the opportunity, would force virtually everything, even his grandmother, into the same shed.' Nearly everyone, however enthusiastic, accepted this was a shed, and that this choice of typology was a surprising choice for an art gallery but not for the architect. *Building Week* ran its review of 7 April under the headline 'Art Shed,' and began; 'Another extrusion of glossy shed slides off the production line of Foster Associates.'[25] But while its iconography was certainly unsettling, the building's uncompromising approach won over the art establishment. An editorial in *The Burlington Magazine* admitted that it 'does look a little like an aircraft hanger, and it does not photograph well,' while *Art Monthly* felt that it 'might well be mistaken for a train station'.[26] Nearly all, however, were swayed by its technological ambition. *The Burlington Magazine* declared that, 'to look upon it as a somehow unworthy home for the arts is entirely to miss the refreshingly changed emphasis of contemporary design. In the Sainsbury Centre much of the

Reception

↓

Shop
Link
Education Studio
Reserve Collection
Lower Gallery
Crescent Wing Reception

ingenuity and brain-work has gone into complex methods of altering light and heat levels, adjusted from a control panel that is like the flight deck of a modern jet.'[27] For *The Burlington Magazine*, a genuinely technological design reminiscent of an aeroplane was clearly to be judged by different criteria from that applied to a 'conventional' building. Sutherland Lyall, writing in *New Society*, perhaps came closest to articulating the widespread appeal of the building when he wrote that the automated louvres of the Sainsbury Centre held 'the same fascination as those press-button machines in the Science Museum.'[28]

The limitations of this brave new technology were discovered when the insulation in the innovative cladding panels failed and had to be replaced in 1988 by the Sainsbury Foundation. But the visual association of Foster with a slick, beautifully detailed solution reminiscent of industrial engineering remained. The meticulous design of the Pompidou Centre and the Sainsbury Centre reminded people of the precision engineering of other types of design. Fuller's idea of technology transfer is employed in the manufacture of both – the pressed aluminium cladding, for example, on the Sainsbury Centre was derived from the car industry. But more importantly these buildings left people with the intoxicating idea that they were the architectural manifestation of the same technological revolution that allowed them

to fly from London to New York on Concorde and arrive before they set off.

When Foster showed the Sainsbury Centre to Buckminster Fuller, he was thrown by Fuller's question, 'how much does it weigh?' Foster found out that the concrete basement, which was only 8 per cent of the volume of the gallery space, weighed 80 per cent of the total. In comparison the main building was built far more quickly than the basement and for half the cost. Foster's central conclusion from the Sainsbury Centre, despite the flurry of interest in its iconography, was a purely technical (and ultimately academic) question that followed the precepts of the master, Fuller.[29]

For both the Pompidou and Sainsbury Centres the production and servicing of a large open space was certainly not the only practical solution to their individual briefs. But their authors were primarily concerned with the provision of a neutral volume. Neither architect would determine the functions of their spaces because they were so committed to the ideal of flexibility. In each case the shed was simply the form that resulted from an exercise in diagrammatic thinking in which the provision of a neutral rectangle of space was paramount.

Rogers frequently chooses to make a visual feature out of his servicing whereas Foster prefers to cover services in sleek cladding. But this distinction ignores the much greater similarities in their approach. Foster took a hangar structure that wrapped the building and

was itself clad. Piano and Rogers exposed not only the primary structure but all its circulation and duct systems. There are obvious technical difficulties involved in doing so and while both buildings have had to be re-clad, the exposed services and external pedestrian escalator of the Pompidou Centre have made it a more complex problem. But neither building was designed as a permanent monument. For example, Richard Rogers, lecturing at the Architectural Association before the Pompidou was built, reputedly claimed that he and Piano were building 'for thirty years'. Today, the Pompidou Centre is thirty years old.

The Sainsbury Centre was from the outset a simple extruded form. The Pompidou Centre, by contrast, is a multi-storey building with a mass of complex shapes on the outside. But it was also conceived as a neutral oblong of flexible space in which the floors could have been moved up or down or even taken out. Certainly both buildings were then consciously styled, and in different ways, but both are the product of a common diagrammatic approach to design which unleashed the potential for an architecture of simple spaces. They gave architectural integrity to a big shed approach, and provided an ideological justification for a practical solution. In doing so they gave high culture status to one of the simplest and most efficient types of building, and opened up big shed architecture to the rest of their profession.

FOLLOWING SPREAD An 'archway' without an entrance in the design of the Sainsbury Centre – traditional architectural hierarchies were replaced by a diagrammatic strategy.

Because these architects fetishized technology and had built structures that were striking and novel, they were interpreted as contributing to a new architectural language. According to the critic Andrew Peckham, Foster's capacity to persuade us, 'doesn't hinge on the traditional language of architecture, but rather on the language of the modern material world – of industrial production and consumable finishes.'[30] This led to the definition of 'High-Tech'. As Colin Davies has pointed out, its practitioners were united only in their hatred of the term. This was because Piano, Rogers and Foster were not interested in architectural languages at all. Other architects such as Theo Crosby lamented the recognizable elements of an architectural language that were missing in their work. For Crosby, the Sainsbury Centre lacked 'an ordered hierarchy that would make sense of the form – an entrance perhaps which is recognizable, part of a language.' But that simply was not a relevant concern to its designer.

As Rogers himself stated, 'to stand inside and experience the heroic scale and simplicity of the Sainsbury Centre fills me with wonder.' That was what he required of it. That it failed to have a traditional doorway, or that what looked like glorious glazed 'entrances' weren't really ways of getting in at all, was irrelevant.

For those who already understood that these buildings were 'sheds' and 'sheds' was 'where it's at' the response was much more muted. Archigram architect Ron Herron found the detailing of the Pompidou Centre a distraction and recognized that the diagrammatic strategy was only half implemented: 'This version of the much-loved "well-serviced shed", although sophisticated, quite beautiful and a much-needed built model, suffers, as does its predecessors, from being over-concerned with dazzling us with its display of environmental hardware and technological symbols – the super-cool "well-serviced shed" has still to be achieved.'

Fellow Archigram member Peter Cook, writing about the Sainsbury Centre in *Architectural Review*, was excited by the project but similarly felt it could have gone further. He did not see it as an aberration from a conventional architectural path but as part of the general search for the 'well-serviced shed' prophesized by Reyner Banham. While 'the original inspiration of the 1960s technological shed was that it could be flexible…one has the suspicion that this remains more of a monumental than a dynamic shed.' Cook felt that it did succeed in drawing a line under architectural languages and traditions and, 'introduced us to the idea, if not the reality, of the shimmering tube.'[31] Ultimately it was with disappointment that Cook concluded that, 'this is not yet the ultimate cool tube. But it comes tantalizingly close to being so.' For some the age of the diagrammatic shed, emerging in the work of Rogers, Piano and Foster, had only just begun.

EXHIBITION

EXHIBITION
Contents and Purpose

Perhaps the most literal building-as-container, the original 'neutral shed', has always been the exhibition building. These are flexible containers designed to accommodate different events of short duration. They house enormous numbers of people for short periods of time and keep them warm or cool, but they have to do little else.

The first building of this kind was the Crystal Palace designed by Joseph Paxton for the original Great Exhibition held in London in 1851. Paxton was not an architect but an engineer and landscape gardener. He had been working on a conservatory at Chatsworth House in Derbyshire when the competition to design the main exhibition structure was announced. Unlike a traditional building this structure had to be erected and then taken down very quickly since it would occupy only a temporary site in Hyde Park. All the competition entries failed to show how this could be done and the committee was forced to consider other options. Paxton hastily designed an iron and timber structure laid out in bays and clad in glass. Neither its structure nor its choice of materials was particularly novel, but the process of its construction – combining prefabrication, standardization and dry-frame construction – was unprecedented.

Paxton's insight was to recognize the potential for new industrial techniques to solve architectural problems. He understood that a strategy would have to be devised that not only controlled the building's construction but also the entire manufacturing process and all of its constituent components. However, Paxton could not have foreseen the aesthetic impact of his logistical vision. A correspondent for *The Times* declared that: 'An entirely novel order of architecture, producing, by means of unrivalled mechanical ingenuity, the most marvellous and beautiful effects, sprang into existence to provide a building.'[1] The Crystal Palace was particularly striking because it was entirely glazed, allowing the public to appreciate the ingenuity of the structure and the repetition of its elements. Enormously influential, it helped foster the belief that the most technologically advanced solution would also prove to be the most beautiful.

While the Crystal Palace was beautiful, the first genuinely innovative exhibition structure was that of the Galerie des Machines, jointly designed by architect Charles Dutert and engineer Victor Contamin for the Paris Exhibition of 1889. An early example of the use of structural steel rather than iron, it spanned a colossal 114 metres (374 feet), dwarfing the previous record of 73 metres (240 feet) held by the span of St Pancras Station. Like the Crystal Palace its outer walls were glazed, giving a clear impression of the structure's simplicity. A series of huge arches, each made up of three separate pieces connected by hinged joints, illustrated the scale of forces at work. One hinge sat at the arch's apex and the other two connected the arch directly to the ground. The Galerie des Machines also established the departure point between the actual mechanics of construction and how a layman might view them, since locating the hinged joints near the ground meant that the structure thinned at precisely the point at which it might be expected to thicken. While this building was taken down in 1910, the Eiffel Tower, built for the same exhibition, gives us a sense of its scale.

The Great Exhibitions were enormously popular. In the last half of the 19th century

hundreds of millions of people visited over fifty sites around the world. In 1893, 27 million visitors attended the World's Columbian Exposition in Chicago alone, and thanks to the recent invention of photography the number of people influenced at second hand would have been many times higher. While these exhibitions were justified as exemplars of 'progress', a popular idea in the 19th century, they were also instrumental in establishing

consumer societies in Europe and the United States. Business leaders were involved in their planning, and commercial values underpinned the national and cultural rhetoric. As Edward Bellamy, a visitor to the World's Columbian Exposition, noted, the 'underlying motive of the whole exhibition, under a sham pretence of patriotism is business, advertising with a view to individual money-making.'[12] This association remains with the 'Great Exhibitions' or 'World's

Fairs' that continue to be held today. These are more commonly described as 'Expos', and an Expo exhibit now consists of an exposition of technological and cultural achievement paid for by a corporation.

World Fairs also spawned more explicitly commercial trade fairs, where particular industries meet to do business. These provide a constant international market for groups of exhibition buildings close to transport links.

But unlike the idealistic ambitions of Expos, the quality of the architecture of trade fair buildings is rarely a priority. Instead the size of their column-free clear spans and total capacities has become the competitive tender.

The German city of Hanover already had the biggest permanent trade fair site in the world when it was chosen as the site for the millennial Expo of 2000. This was to be the first Expo held in Germany and was supposed to act as a forum to improve Germany's image abroad.[3] It cost $1.6 billion and its theme was 'Humankind-Nature-Technology'. Prior to the event the architect and academic Thomas Herzog had been commissioned to design **Hall 26**, a new hall that would set the standard for future development on the site. Since his university dissertation on pneumatic structures in 1972, Herzog has collaborated with various research bodies to apply innovative engineering techniques to architecture.[4] As such, his appointment was intended to establish the qualities to which an 'Expo standard' exhibition hall should aspire.

Hall 26 covers a 220-metre by 115-metre (722-foot by 377-foot) footprint with three tensile roof structures suspended between 29-metre (95-foot) high steel trestle masts. The roofs hang in sloping curves from fixed horizontal members and give the building a

HANOVER HALL 26
LEFT Tensile roof structures hang from steel trestle masts.

HANOVER HALL 26
BELOW A glass air-duct/walkway runs between the trestle masts.

serrated profile similar to that of the rows of north-facing windows in early factories, but on a giant scale. The roofs are made up of prefabricated composite timber panels. These contain a vapour barrier, thermal insulation and a layer of gravel that increases the weight of the roof sufficiently to resist suction forces caused by the wind. The undersides of the panels are bolted directly to flat steel members, 300 millimetres by 40 millimetres (12 by 1.6 inches)

in section, that support the panels across the 55-metre (180-foot) span. Together they form a single structural sheet, which absorbs the wind loads from the façades and transfers them to the masts below.

The building's profile also reflects its environmental strategy. The floor of the building had to be designed to take very heavy loads due to the frequent movement of forklift trucks and occasionally very heavy display items.

Consequently it would have been impossible to set servicing within it. Herzog's solution was to introduce fresh air at a height of 4.7 metres (15 feet) from a glass tube that runs between the trusses, thus distributing it evenly across the floor. In the summer the air ducts expel cool air, which drops down as warmer air is expelled via flaps at the three roof ridges creating a chimney effect. In winter, warm air is released through the same ducts.

HANOVER HALL 8/9
BELOW Hall 8 lies below the staircase that leads across a motorway to the other half of the Expo site.

HANOVER HALL 8/9
OPPOSITE Under the ridge of each roof suspension cables tie the load to the ground.

Six cubes protrude through the building's perimeter providing ancillary services such as toilets, catering and maintenance facilities. These are clad in timber outside but left as fair-faced concrete inside. The entire structure was built in thirty-nine weeks and was completed in 1996.

Another new hall, **Hall 8/9**, was commissioned for the Expo through a competition process won by architects von Gerkan, Marg + Partners (GMP). GMP are a German practice who appear to have as many prestigious infrastructure-scale architectural projects in Germany as Foster and Partners have in the UK. The project that established their reputation was the Berlin-Tegel Airport, which they designed using a unique drive-in strategy with stacked parking, an original approach that used a simple diagram based on access. Throughout their careers Meinhard von Gerkan and Volkwin Marg have designed simple diagrammatic solutions to architectural problems crafted in engineered-aesthetic details. Hall 8/9 provided not only a column-free space the size of four football fields, but also a

staircase leading over the motorway footbridge that connected both sides of the exhibition site. Underneath the staircase the smaller Hall 8 connected Hall 9 to the existing Hall 7. Hall 9, like Hall 26, is a suspended construction but built on a smaller, more numerous, module. Its pagoda-like curved roofs cover a space 137.5 metres by 237.5 metres (451 feet by 780 feet) supported on trusses placed 45 metres (148 feet) apart. Each truss functions like a separate suspension bridge. A series of masts support four load-bearing cables, which are then extended along struts that form either end of the frame, and are finally anchored into reinforced footings. The roof steels are simply lined with wooden boxes, which also contain light fittings and air-ducts. As at Hall 26, the contiguous boxes form a curved plate transferring east–west horizontal loads to the main girders and from the girders into the main cables.

Largely a product of prefabrication, Hall 9's masthead and stays (which are approximately 7.5 metres (25 feet) tall, 25 metres (82 feet) long, and weigh up to 50 tonnes) arrived on site already welded together. They were then erected

BELOW AND OPPOSITE Inside, a column-free space the size of four football fields is supported by trusses that function like suspension bridges.

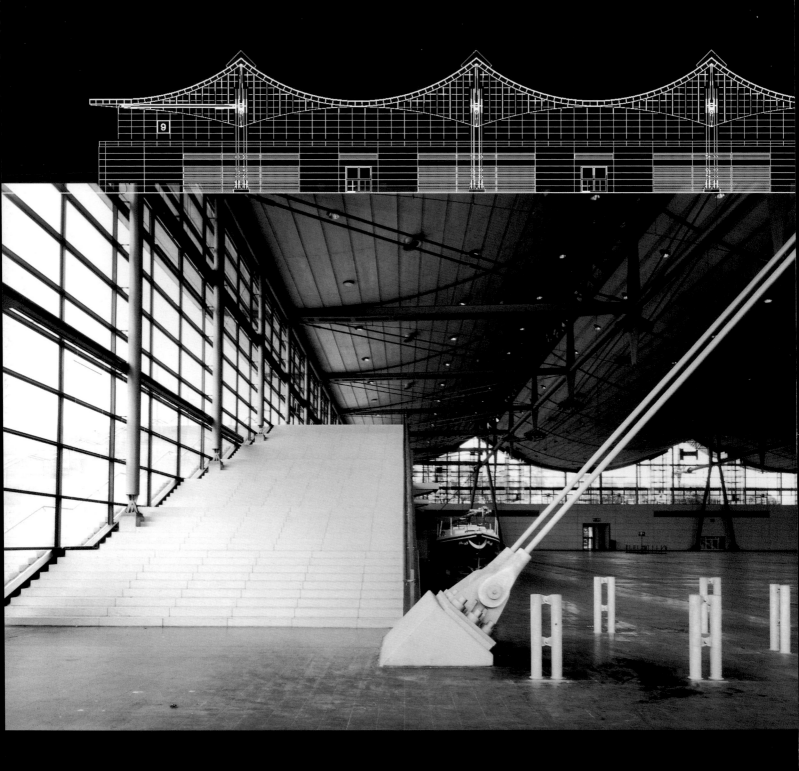

HANOVER HALL 8/9
ABOVE Hanging roof steels are lined with wooden boxes containing light fittings and air-ducts.

HANOVER HALL 8/9
OPPOSITE A mezzanine level extends around three sides of the building's perimeter.

with cranes and cablestayed. Hall 8/9 was built swiftly, taking only eleven weeks to erect the steel structure and five weeks to install the 1,584 wooden boxes.

The quality of Hanover's new halls did not, however, ensure the success of Expo 2000. After Germany's reunification Hanover was a city inexorably drifting out of the cultural limelight as Berlin moved centre stage, and while there were more participants than ever before, with contributions from 174 nations, the financial commitment of the major industrialized nations was waning. Significantly there was no American pavilion. The existing trade fair facilities also became a mixed blessing. The idea of staging exhibits inside was meant to save exhibitors the expense of building their own pavilions, but it proved less attractive for the participants, provided a diminished sense of spectacle and,

with commercial trade fair prices, was still not cheap. Forty-nine nations therefore chose to build their own external pavilions, and the result was an enormous characterless site straddling a motorway in a relatively inhospitable climate. Forty-one million visitors were predicted, but only 18.1 million attended, resulting in considerable financial loss.

Hanover's difficulties may be part of a wider malaise. The concept of a World Fair bringing together examples of national products from all over the globe now appears to be under threat. The proliferation of visual media has made it much harder for exhibitions to surprise, and with the expansion in cheap air travel a much greater array of things can be experienced first hand. Nonetheless, when the millennium was celebrated in London, the city chose to celebrate with a high-profile exhibition. The idea

that this should be housed in a single dome
originated in sketches done by Mike Davies of
the Richard Rogers Partnership. Upon visiting
the chosen site at Greenwich on a freezing
winter morning, Davies quickly recognized why
no external exhibition had been mounted in
Britain during the middle of winter. As a
consequence he sought a solution that housed
an unknown series of exhibitions under a
single roof. The other advantage of a single
all-encompassing structure was that separate
programmes for the construction of the building
and the exhibits could run concurrently,
unhindered by each other.

The **Millennium Dome** is not actually a
dome but a net structure made up of 70
kilometres (43.5 miles) of high-strength cabling
supported by twelve steel masts each 100
metres (328 feet) long. It has an overall
diameter of 365 metres (1,197 feet), an internal
diameter of 320 metres (1,050 feet) and a 1-
kilometre (.62-mile) circumference. Despite
being a very shallow form the space rises to 50
metres (164 feet) in the centre and encloses a
ground-floor area of 100,000 square metres (1.1
million square feet), with a total volume of 2.2
million cubic metres (78 million cubic feet).

Cable-net structures are quick and easy to
build and can span enormous distances in the
same manner as suspension bridges. More
difficult to calculate are the effects 'non-
uniform applied loads' – such as wind, rain and
snow – have on the structure. Being circular the

MILLENNIUM DOME

OPPOSITE Built on the Meridian Line in Greenwich, the Dome's twelve masts refer to the twelve months of the year, and hours of the clock face.

Millennium Dome is a very efficient structure both in terms of loading and repetition of elements and works in a system comparable to six nesting suspension bridges. Most remarkable is its answer to Buckminster Fuller's criterion of efficiency – all the cables, all the fabric and all the masts weigh less than a 13-metre (43-foot) cube of water.

The structural engineer Buro Happold calculated the loads using 'Tensyl' software devised to analyse tension structures. The cigar shape of the masts reflects their function as compression members, but their circumference, which determines the load they can support, was limited by transportation requirements. Manufactured in sections by Watson Steel of Bolton they were then assembled on site. Placed on pyramid bases, they are constructed on the redundancy principle that if one of the four legs fails the mast continues to be supported. At the apex of the dome 72 radial cables are joined together by a cable ring made up of seven separate cables. As the whole roof would collapse if this broke, the cable ring is designed so that even if six cables fail the ring still holds.

The building was very cheap, costing only £43 million ($US80 million) for the ground works, perimeter wall, masts, cable net structure and roof fabric. It was delivered in fifteen months and under-budget. The exhibition inside, however, was widely regarded as a fiasco. The Dome was filled by a series of exhibits

grouped into themed zones. These were designed by a variety of architects and some were imaginative, but the enterprise as a whole lacked a clear purpose. The Great Exhibition of 1851 was an expression of the cultural products of the Industrial Revolution, seen against a backdrop of imperial pomp. The 1951 Festival of Britain was intended to boost morale for a tired but optimistic nation recovering from the Second World War. But the contents of the Millennium Dome were neither didactic nor entertaining and seemed only to combine the disadvantages of either approach. What was clear was that the South Kensington museums, the direct products of the 1851 Great Exhibition, could still provide a much more interesting and enjoyable day out. As The Observer stated on 30 January 2000, 'The Dome, built to re-energize the nation, raise the self-esteem of its people and enhance the nation's standing, is a flop.'[5] What was worse was that no satisfactory plan was prepared for what the building would be after December 2000.

While grand exhibition buildings, such as the Dome, often struggle, more anonymous trade fair buildings continue to be built in large numbers. Trade fairs are international events and as a consequence trade fair grounds in different countries are in direct competition. As a prominent criterion of choice is the uninterrupted single space their buildings provide, many exhibition halls are designed with enormous spans.

These spans allow stand designers to plan schemes that can be re-erected in a number of exhibition venues worldwide and whose sight lines are free from disruptive columns. Aesthetically, this has resulted in a style of simple exhibition building in which a vast roof structure towers overhead. **Hall 2** and Hall 4 in Hanover are both buildings of this type. Hall 2, which opened in 1993, was designed by Bertram, Bünemann + Partner. Here, 12,000 square metres (130,000 square feet) are clear-spanned by a roof that combines a bow-shaped form constructed in space-frame trusses, which are then tied down by steel cables supported by concrete columns. By contrast, Hall 4, built by GMP in 1996, has visible elliptical bow-string trusses with cable-ties that are reputedly inspired by Hanover's great classical architect Georg Ludwig Friedrich Laves who devised this 'fish belly' profile for use in bridge construction. The disadvantage of this system is that the morass of ties visually interfere, detracting from an otherwise powerful sense of volume, and it is the simpler structure of Hall 2 that is the more satisfying.

The quest for ever-larger clear spans to seduce prospective clients led Nicholas Grimshaw and Partners (NGP) to design the enormous **Messehalle 3** at the Frankfurt trade fair. Taught at the Architectural Association when it was under the influence of Archigram and Cedric Price, Grimshaw shares one of their most cherished principles[6] – that people have a

fundamental right to manipulate their surroundings.[7] Grimshaw's student thesis was published in *Archigram* in 1965, and in it he stated the classic position of the technological optimist: 'It is my hope that it is not buildings we will be designing in the future, it is organisms capable of variation and adaptation within as large a range as the technology of the minute permits.'[8]

For fifteen years Grimshaw worked in partnership with architect Terry Farrell. During this time he produced one of the first prefabricated pod structures, a service tower that plugged into a refurbished building in Sussex Gardens, West London, in the manner of an Archigram project. Since setting up his own practice, Grimshaw's career has followed that of Foster and Rogers with work that has been described as 'High-Tech'. Like them he has

favoured an engineered-architectural approach with an emphasis on prefabrication, lightweight construction and original detailing. Grimshaw's buildings explicitly reveal their industrial design influences and the architect he most admires is Jean Prouvé, who was not an architect by training but an industrial designer. Grimshaw also sees himself as working within an engineering tradition that passes back beyond Prouvé to Paxton. Grimshaw has spoken glowingly about the contribution of Paxton's Crystal Palace to architecture. Specifically it is Paxton's diagrammatic approach and logistical strategy that he admires. According to early apologist Colin Amery, Grimshaw 'reveres Paxton, whose Crystal Palace of 1851 he points out as an example of an initial conceptual sketch carried through almost unaltered into the completed building'.[9] Indeed, Amery believes

that Grimshaw may be placed in a tradition that can be traced right back to the world's first cast-iron bridge at Coalbrookdale in 1776.[10] Messehalle 3 marks a return to a fairly functionalist brief for Nicholas Grimshaw and Partners in the manner of their early designs for factories. The trade fair site at Frankfurt has a higher profile than others partly because it is unusually close to the centre of the city. The competition for Messehalle 3 was to design a hall on a prominent location to the south side of the Agora, a major public space in the exhibition area. It would also have to be completed in eighteen months in order to house the International Motor Show of September 2001.

Nicholas Grimshaw and Partners intensified the drama inherent in a long-span roof by choosing to span the longer east–west axis. This allowed the north façade onto the square to be fully glazed and uncluttered by structure. The roof is a folded plate that follows a wave-like profile made up of concave and convex elements. It spans 165 metres (541 feet), one of the largest clear spans in Europe. Technically the concave sections are tubular gridshells, and the lower convex sections anticlastic tensile nets. Both are constructed from lengths of straight steel tubes welded into facets to make up the curves. The thickness of these tubes varies according to the differing stresses they receive as a consequence of their location. This sinuous section stiffens the roof as a whole as well as giving it a much more expressive appearance.

The surface of the roof is made up of prefabricated panels constructed on site with an in-built twist in order to accommodate the curving profile. The repetitive nature of the structure meant that only six different types of panel were required. Twelve steel A-frames buttress the roof and crash dramatically through the service wings that sit on either side of the building. These wings are five-storey concrete structures that house conference and office facilities, kitchens and toilets. They also provide lateral restraint to the A-frames. Continuous clearstorey glazing above the monopitch roofs of the service wings provides ample light deep into the plan and ensures that the roof 'hovers' visually over the building. The façade is further articulated by pyramidal ventilation couls that

MESSEHALLE 3, FRANKFURT
OPPOSITE Detail of the south façade.

MESSEHALLE 3, FRANKFURT
BELOW The final set of 'A'-frames supporting the
roof are wholly visible on the outside of
the building.

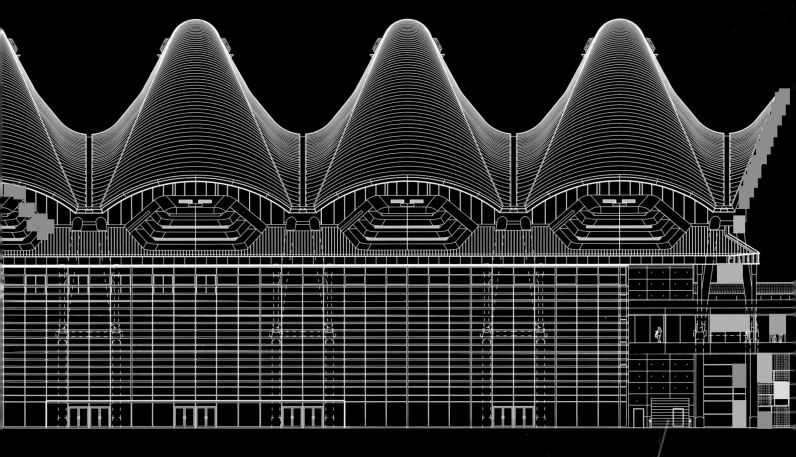

MESSEHALLE 3, FRANKFURT
LEFT The folded plate structure combines concave tubular gridshells and convex anticlastic tensile nets.

MESSEHALLE 3, FRANKFURT
RIGHT A more conventional lower hall supports the floor of the clear-span hall.

MESSEHALLE 3, FRANKFURT
BELOW Service wings on either side provide lateral
restraint to the A-frames that penetrate them.

MESSEHALLE 3, FRANKFURT
RIGHT The design of the rear escape stairs
of Messehalle 3 illustrates its finely
engineered approach.

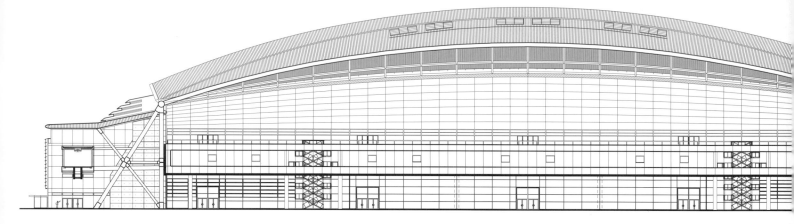

'plug in' to the glazing, continuing the curved roof profile onto the service-wings.

A 4-metre (12-foot) service zone sits between this open-span exhibition space and the columned hall that lies beneath it. This zone contains air conditioning, sewage and high-voltage power to service both floors and is large enough to provide a fire escape tunnel and maintenance access.

Grimshaw recognized the tendency of exhibition halls towards anonymity and while he has explained the design solely in terms of its efficiency and structural daring, it is also a deliberately evocative interior. The large-span hall, with its curving structural ribcage, has visual echoes of H. R. Giger's sets for the series of *Alien* films. This effect is intensified rather than diminished by the curved boons that sit within the arches providing lighting and the air handling plant. Nicholas Grimshaw and Partners have answered the substantial requirements of the design brief with an engineered solution, but Messehalle 3 is also a deliberately aestheticized form.

Exhibition buildings are now adjuncts of transport systems. Since they could effectively be anywhere – the draw is the contents – the determining factor is often how easily the site may be reached. At a 1986 meeting in Lille Town Hall, British Prime Minister Margaret Thatcher and President François Mitterrand of France finalized plans to build the Channel Tunnel.

GRAND PALAIS

ABOVE The back of banked seating is shown on the outside of the Grand Palais' 'Zenith'.

GRAND PALAIS

OPPOSITE The foyer entrance leading to the exhibition hall.

LEFT OMA's frugal aesthetic – entrance to
the car park below the Grand Palais.

The following year France, Belgium, Holland
and Germany signed up to an agreement to co-
develop a North European Train à Grande Vitesse
(TGV) network. Local politicians lobbied to get
the Brussels–Paris line to interchange at the old
industrial city of Lille and, as a result, it became
the key interchange for the Channel Tunnel
trains linking Paris, Brussels and London. It also
instigated the rapid creation of a whole new
chunk of Lille to take advantage of these new
communications.

In 1988 architect Rem Koolhaas of the
Office for Metropolitan Architecture (OMA) was
appointed chief architect and masterplanner of
the new 'Euralille' urban development. OMA
were then commissioned to design the largest
structure in the complex, the Grand Palais.

The site of the Grand Palais (or
'Congrexpo') is triangular, located between the
rail tracks of the existing Lille station and two
major roads. The new building contains a 20,000
square metre (215,000 square foot) expo hall, a
conference centre with three auditoria, and a
music venue for 5,000. All are located in a single
container, oval in plan, which sits above a 1,300-
space car park.

Looking at the building's exterior, the very
disparate forms of all three sections of the
building are abutted without visual connections
across the façade. The concert hall, or 'Zenith',
occupies the north end. 'Zenith' refers to a
French colloquial term for a multi-purpose hall,
generally used as a music venue. Here the

auditorium sits in the broad bottom chunk of
the oval plan, with the stage backing onto a flat
wall that abuts the rest of the complex. The
banks of tiered seating form its curved façade.
Constructed using a faceted formwork system
based on a standard 2- by 1.2-metre (6- by 4-
foot) plywood sheet, it was much quicker
and cheaper than following the geometry
exactly and suited OMA's frugal aesthetic.
A single 70-metre (230-foot) transverse primary
truss supports the roof, 5.4 metres (18 feet) deep
in its thickest part. This then supports a series
of secondary trusses that run from it to the edge
of the ovoid roof. The whole system is designed
to suspend loads of up to twenty tonnes over
the stage.

The Congress Conference Centre forms a
rectangle in the middle of the plan, and contains
20,000 square metres (215,000 square feet) over
five floors. It includes three theatres (seating
1,500, 500 and 320 respectively) and is made up
of a concrete structure, part pre-cast and part
cast in situ.

At the south end sits an Exhibition Centre,
which subdivides into three areas, each
approximately 48 metres wide by 150 metres
long (157 by 492 feet). The roof is unusual. OMA
determined that it should be a convex curved
dish shape rising towards the perimeter, and
as a result the length of columns vary between
9 and 19 metres (29 and 62 feet). Engineers,
Arup, were charged with designing the structure
of the roof. While this would have been logical
to mould this shape in concrete, the economics
of such a large-span roof determined that it
should be steel-framed. So Arup approximated
a smooth soffit with a slatted ceiling made out
of timber strips.

GRAND PALAIS
RIGHT Interior of 'Zenith' music venue.

GRAND PALAIS
FOLLOWING SPREAD OMA's visual tricks can be seen
at the Congress Conference Centre
where the roof slab reaches down
to the ground.

Koolhaas used the Grand Palais to make
an enthusiastic case for buildings of extreme
size. While this project appeared in a book
entitled *S,M,L,XL*, Koolhaas's enthusiasms were
all about 'Bigness'. Here the Grand Palais was
publicized in a fanfare of zeitgeistian publicity
explaining how architecture was the least
important part of such a project. It suggested
that 'Bigness' was a new urban phenomenon
that changed the rules regarding architectural
design.

As critic Peter Davey complained,
Koolhaas's book was, 'largely an uncritical hymn
to the totally impersonal values of the global
market',[11] and a particularly smug hymn at that,
as it praised what was a very profitable situation
for OMA. Yet Koolhaas had at least recognized
that big sheds were a worldwide phenomenon.
He saw that the crassness of the big shed
solution was generated by both economics
and politics.

While OMA chose to emphasize the cheap
approximations necessary in such a huge but
inexpensive building, architect Bernard Tschumi
took a different approach. The **Zenith** built at
Rouen was the tenth such structure to be
constructed in France. Completed in only
thirteen months, it followed a deadline set
by local elections in March 2001, a hasty
present to a fickle electorate.

Tschumi is an academic architect whose
early exploratory work was on paper, first at the
Architectural Association in London, and then at

Columbia University in New York. He is
associated with an architectural style that has
been labelled 'deconstructivist' that, like 'High-
Tech', united its members only in antipathy
towards the term.

Tschumi's Zenith was built on a site on the
city's outskirts visible from the A13 motorway to
Paris. It consists of two separate but connected
buildings with different characters: a 7,000-seat
music venue and a 7,000-square metre (75,000
square foot) exhibition hall.

The exhibition hall is a simple rectangular
block, but the scheme derives its identity from
the tyre-shaped curves that surround the
auditorium. As with Koolhaas's site at Lille, the
auditorium is designed to serve as a popular
music venue. Its curve is derived from two
separate radii so that the curve of seating
becomes tighter to the east. This allows the

seating to be easily divided up and reconfigured
to satisfy the particular requirements of
individual events. The floor of the auditorium is
made up of concrete steps that can be clearly
seen through transparent plastic seats, and the
effect is reminiscent of the theatres of classical
Greece and Rome.

To the south, around the concrete-walled
auditorium, is a second skin of corrugated steel
that encloses an entrance and circulation space.
It also provides necessary acoustic separation.
At the base of the torus a vertical layer of glazing
sits back from the ribs creating a visual break
that makes the torus seem to 'float' visually.

A full-height glazed wall provides an
entrance to the auditorium, lying between these
steel toruses like the opening in a snail's shell.
Within, there are fifteen entrances to the
auditorium, accessed by a range of ramps

ZENITH

ABOVE Clear seats allow the concrete steps
to be seen, reminiscent of a Greek or
Roman theatre.

ZENITH

OPPOSITE Entranceway from interior.

and stairs. The idea is that the building can be emptied within ten minutes of the end of the show. Above the toruses three suspension masts keep the auditorium column-free while giving the building a recognizable presence from the motorway.

In general, exhibition buildings – like shopping centres – exploit the low land costs on the outskirts of the city. A notable exception has been built in the centre of one of the world's largest and most expensive conurbations. The **Tokyo International Forum** was built in 1996 in the heart of Tokyo at a total cost of $US1.5 billion. Commissioned by the Tokyo Municipal Government it was conceived as a centre for cultural exchange that would establish a symbol of Japan's importance in international trade. According to former governor Sunichi Suzuki it envisaged a place 'where citizens of Tokyo can

meet with other peoples from all over the world.'[12] A 2.7-hectare (6.7-acre) site was chosen in the city's Central Business District, not far from the central railway station. The government held Japan's second international competition in 1989. Unlike the competition for Kansai Airport where practices were invited, this was open to anyone and entries would be judged anonymously.

The competition was won by the US-based architectural practice of Rafael Viñoly. Their scheme was successful because it fitted a colossal amount of floorspace within the constraints of the site. To the west the plan respected the existing city blocks by extending them into four boxy auditoriums. These neutral grey boxes, clad in granite and aluminium, fit neatly into the corporate architecture of the Marunouchi financial district. To the east the

remaining area was bounded by the rail tracks
that ran diagonally across the site. Here Rafael
Viñoly Architects' submission utilized the space
that remained by defining an elliptical sliver as
the entrance hall to the complex. This takes the
curved site boundary created by the curve of
the Japan Railways (JR) railway tracks and then
mirrored it to form an ellipse. This shape is
extruded in a single-storey glass hall over 60
metres (197 feet) tall. The latest manifestation
of the great glass hall (that began with Paxton's
Crystal Palace), the forum is 30 metres (98 feet)
at its widest and 210 metres (689 feet) in
length. In addition to the main lobby it houses
two exhibition areas, a conference centre,
administrative offices and catering facilities.

Every attempt has been made to make
the glass hall as unsettling a space as possible.
In the competition scheme the structure was
daring but still much more conservative than it
is now. Twelve columns ran along the central
axis supporting the 210-metre (689-foot)
structure. After the competition was won,
however, structural engineer Kunio Watanabe of
Tokyo-based Structural Design Group suggested
a more radical alternative. His idea was to
support the structure on just two columns at
either end, and tie it down along its perimeter.
Consequently, the entire edifice is held up by
two columns just 4.5 metres (15 feet) thick at
their widest and taper to 1.3 metres (4 feet)
where they meet the ground and the roof.
Between them is a 124-metre (407-foot) span

supported by an enormous roof truss. What look
like fifty-six upside-down 'arches' actually hold
in position the sixteen tension cables and two
1.5-metre (5-foot) diameter compression
members, which run the entire length of the
roof. Consequently they act as ribs for a truss
that takes the literal shape of a three-
dimensional bending moment diagram.[13]

Huge expanses of glass are uncommon in
Tokyo because of the frequency of earthquakes.
Viñoly blithely claimed that this was 'more for
psychological reasons than engineering'[14] and
designed the west wall 57 metres (187 feet) tall
and fully glazed. The 16-millimetre ($5/8$-inch)
thick laminated glass is hung from the ends of
the 'arches' and stabilized by cable-trusses.
These also serve to tie the roof structure down
in the event of an earthquake. The structure is
buttressed by walkways running around the
building's perimeter. These act as stiffening
ribs to absorb wind loads. Bridges also fly across
the hall at angles, cross-bracing the structure
and giving the space a Piranesian grandeur.
In order to defend against tremors there are no
expansion joints in the building's foundations,
so the bridges act as movement joints attaching
the glass hall to the theatre blocks across the
courtyard. While they are structurally linked to
the theatre blocks, their floors run freely over
the walkways of the glass hall.

Tokyo International Forum was conceived
as a way to advertise the freemarket aspirations
of a city encouraging international trade. But in

many ways the building is closed off. There is
little space on its glass façades to advertise
'what's on', and the inside is remote and
detached from the public spaces around it.
The whole focus of the design is a structural
system that is remarkably daring in Toyko's
seismic context.

It is both the scale and simplicity of
exhibition buildings that continue to provide an
opportunity for grand structures in the manner
of the Crystal Palace. In the case of engineering
purists like Nicholas Grimshaw they chose a
lucid expressive structure. For Koolhaas and
OMA, it was the opportunity for a diatribe on
economics and urbanism. For Viñoly it was the
grand span itself, a gesture of overwhelming
engineering confidence, that provides the
architectural statement.

INDUSTRY

INDUSTRY
Manufacture and Storage

Industry, of all the traditional sources of architectural patronage, tends to produce simple utilitarian buildings. This is because industrial buildings are mainly inhabited not by people but by materials and processes. It was this utilitarian character that, during the early years of the 20th century, attracted the first generation of modern architects. Industrial buildings rarely warranted ornament, and so displayed fewer characteristics of the existing architectural styles. At the same time the modernists, uninterested in the application of historical grammars, actively sought industrial commissions less appealing to their more traditional colleagues. The result was that buildings such as Peter Behrens's AEG Turbine Factory and Walter Gropius's Fagus Works had an enormous influence on the development of the Modern Movement.

Central to the Modern Movement's ethos was the principle that a building's structure should be clearly expressed. But many 19th-century buildings are actually more lucid expressions of structure than the industrial buildings of the early modernists. A direct comparison of Behrens's AEG Turbine Factory (1908–1909) and Dutert and Contamin's Galerie des Machines in Paris (1889), for example, reveals their fundamental structural similarity. Both buildings are based on an arch with three hinged joints. But while Behrens hid his building behind what appeared to be masonry walls (marked by classical striations), its arches

seemingly supported by the masonry, the Galerie des Machines was fully glazed. Its aggressive steel form, clearly pin-jointed at ground level, showed that the structure needed to flex and move. Behrens was trying to co-opt industrial motifs into a traditional architectural language, and still sought the authority of the classical tradition; twenty years earlier Dutert and Contamin had felt no such compunction.

While the early modernists talked a lot about the inspiration of industry, their buildings actually had the effect of taking technology as a theme and making it a formal language. During the same period, however, industrial buildings were being erected that were so dominated by their structural requirements that they did not seem to have a conventional architectural aspect at all. Some of the earliest buildings to display real engineering prowess were the hangars where airships were built, serviced and stored. These hangars first appeared during the massive expansion of lighter-than-air travel in the 1910s. Germany was at the forefront and established a successful airship passenger service operated by a company called DELAG (Deutsche Luftschiffahrt Aktien Gesellschaft). During the 1930s DELAG even ran inter-continental services to North and South America, before the entire enterprise was dramatically curtailed by the Hindenberg disaster of 6 May 1937.

It would be sixty years before any attempt was made to re-establish an airship network.

Once again it was a German company, Cargolifter AG, that explored the possibilities of using lighter-than-air travel to provide something other than portable advertising. Cargolifter's intention was to use a new range of helium-filled 'blimps' (airships without rigid skeletons) to transport freight of up to 160 tonnes as far as 10,000 kilometres (6,200 miles). They commissioned Munich-based architects SIAT Architektur & Technik, and structural engineers from Arup to design a hangar in which to make the blimps. This would be called 'CL21', the **Cargolifter Airship Hangar**. A 400-hectare (988-acre) site was found at a former Soviet airfield in Brand, 50 kilometres (31 miles) south of Berlin. It was ideal: flat and sparsely populated but relatively near to a big city. The sandy soil of this Lower Lusatia region could also absorb the high compression rates imposed by a very heavy structure, and was free of ground water problems as it was part of an elevated plateau.

The Cargolifter hangar was designed to allow two CL160 blimps to be built side by side. Because blimps are rounder than Zeppelins (which have structural frameworks), the hangar is correspondingly rounder (and hence higher and wider) but not much longer than previous airship sheds. The architects and engineers drew upon research into lightweight structures done at Stuttgart University during the 1970s and 1980s by Frei Otto and Berthold Burkhardt. They found that the most efficient structure would

CARGOLIFTER AIRSHIP HANGAR
LEFT The squat proportions of the hangar
reflect the rotund shape of the blimps
that were to be built within it.

require five semi-cylindrical, rigid and hinge-less
arches set out at 35-metre (115-foot) centres.
Actually these arches are not perfectly
cylindrical but polygonal, made up of seventeen
straight segments, each 18 metres (59 feet) long.
Each springs from a concrete plinth into which
the entrances are set. These plinths anchor the
structure and prevent lateral movement or
'sliding' caused by the massive wind loads and
thrusts from the arches. Locating the entrances
in them was a technique that dated back to the
airship hangar built by Eugène Freyssinet at Orly
in 1923. The plinth protects visitors from the
dangers of avalanches of snow sliding off the
107-metre (351-foot) high roof.

The steel arches are cross-braced both to
prevent torsional buckling and to buttress the
horizontal loads caused by the opening of
massive doors that lay at either end of the
building. These doors would allow the huge
craft in and out. This is traditionally the most
dangerous moment in airship production
because the large surface area can encourage
the wind to ram the ship into the hangar. As a
result the hangar's longitudinal walls were built
parallel to the prevailing winds. With doors at
either end the airship could enter and leave in
both directions.

The doors are themselves an innovation.
They are made up of six moving and two fixed
sections, mounted on rails, which splay out
from a central pivot. Their arch length is 168
metres (551 feet) and they reach 42 metres

CARGOLIFTER AIRSHIP HANGAR

OPPOSITE The doors are supported by a lattice of
horizontal, vertical and diagonal struts
of identical profile.

CARGOLIFTER AIRSHIP HANGAR

FOLLOWING SPREAD Holiday-makers take in the 5.2 million
cubic metre (184 million cubic foot)
volume from a helium balloon – a sad
reminder of Cargolifter's airship
ambitions.

(138 feet) at their base. This means that they are enormously heavy, a problem relieved by choosing a shell structure to support them. Horizontal, vertical and diagonal struts of an identical profile make up the three-dimensional shell grid. At their bases the doors are stiffened by beams that nest inside each other during opening.

The building was designed during 1997 and 1998 and completed in 2000. Cargolifter released a glossy book to mark its completion. The introduction – entitled 'A vision turns reality' – heralded a glorious new era in lighter-than-air transport and lamented, 'the tendency to moan' that was 'wearisomely familiar in Germany'. Instead it looked to what it saw as 'untapped potential for enthusiasm. The Cargolifter project is proof… The hangar design is now fascinating reality. It has injected a new quality into the Cargolifter project – for now we begin to build our airships.'[1] In July 2002 Cargolifter signed a contract with Boeing to jointly explore 'stratospheric airship concepts' Then they went bust. The hangar was sold to Malaysian cruise-line entrepreneur Colin Au who spent 20 million euros acquiring the building and another 50 million euros turning it into a fantasy tropical holiday resort complete with wave machines, 500 species of animals and 14,000 plants.

Cargolifter Airship Hangar (or Tropical Islands as it is now called) remains the world's largest self-supporting enclosure, containing 5.2 million cubic metres (184 million cubic feet). It would comfortably fit over Berlin's Potsdamer Platz and all its constituent buildings.[2] Cargolifter's hangar represents a key fascination of technologists from Buckminster Fuller to the present day – that of the issue of ever-expanding size. It is a direct consequence of to the desire to harness existing technologies to serve a new purpose, a physical manifestation of an economy of scale. Cargolifter's crash was a reminder that even massive industrial buildings are often still a relatively cheap part of a much more expensive process.

Airbus invested over US$12 billion in the development of their new A380 superjumbo, the world's largest passenger aircraft. The A380's final assembly takes place in the **Jean-Luc Lagardère Building** in Toulouse. The building's footprint is bigger even than that of the Cargolifter hangar (though unlike Cargolifter it is supported by columns), yet it forms only a tiny part of the cost of the project. The unprecedented scale of the A380 has had ramifications for every stage in its manufacture. For political as well as economic reasons, the constituent parts of Airbus aeroplanes are manufactured in different countries around Europe. The sub-assemblies of most models are transported in the world's largest cargo aircraft – the Airbus Beluga – but the sheer scale of the A380 sub-assemblies has made this impossible. These are transported instead by sea and then overland, and this has required the construction of new port facilities and new roads. Since the wings are made in England and Wales, the fuselage in France and Germany, and the tailfins in Spain, transportation costs have been considerable.

The final assembly building is designed to allow engineers to work on three A380s simultaneously. During the process of assembly each plane is brought in at one end and then wheeled out and back into the next bay to face the other way. The A380 covers an area appreciably larger than that of a Boeing 747. As a consequence this building is 490 metres (1,608 feet) long and 250 metres (820 feet) wide, a footprint that covers 10 hectares (25 acres). Each roof section, weighing 8,000 tonnes, was assembled with all its service requirements and hydraulic equipment at ground level and then, in one day, raised to the 46-metre (151-foot) height of the building. It therefore mirrored the manufacturing procedure used for the aircraft themselves.

While the Jean-Luc Lagardère final assembly building is an extreme example of scale – of the kind dwarfed only by the 40-hectare (99-acre) footprint of the Boeing Everett factory in Washington State – very large buildings are also regularly required for the frequent servicing of commercial and military aircraft. Usually these structures are kept in the outlying parts of airports, out of the public eye. But when Lufthansa Technik, the company that services Lufthansa and other airlines, designed

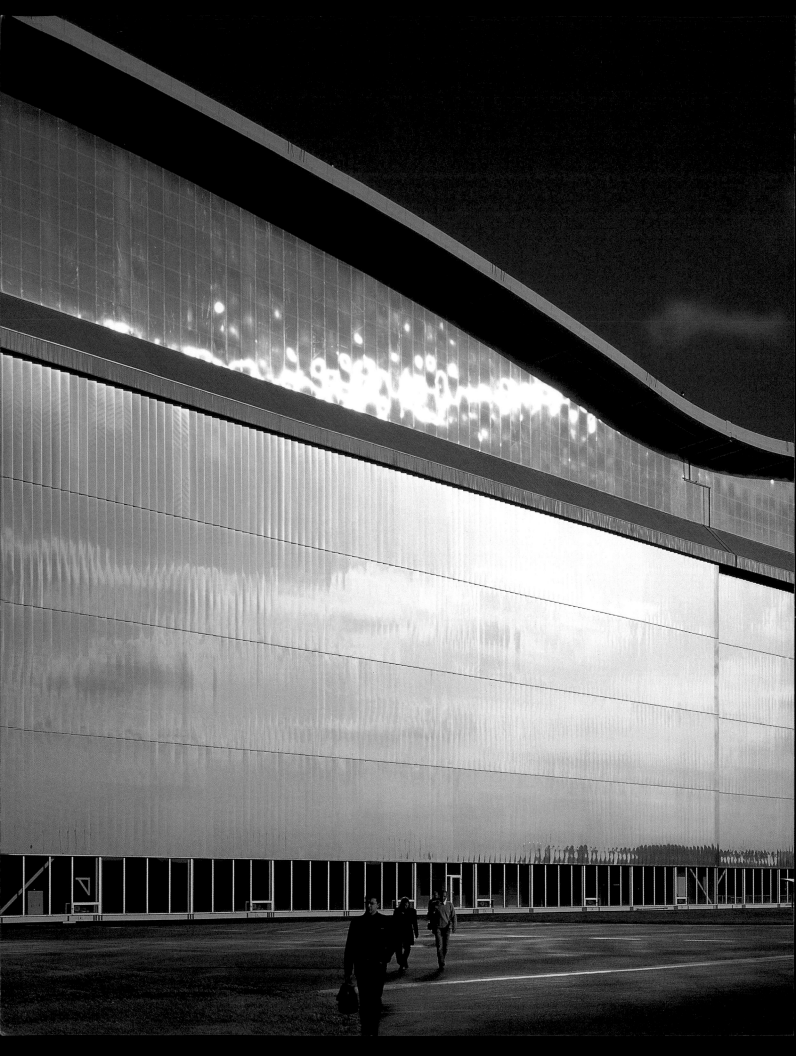

JEAN-LUC LAGARDÈRE BUILDING
PREVIOUS SPREAD Airbus engineers complete their shift
on the A380.

JEAN-LUC LAGARDÈRE BUILDING
RIGHT The roof is designed not only for a
large clear span but also to support
sections of the aircraft.

HAMBURG MAINTENANCE HANGAR
FOLLOWING SPREAD The fully glazed façade allows
passengers a glimpse into what is
required to ensure their safety.

its **Hamburg Maintenance Hangar** for Boeing
747s, it chose to make the building both public
and visually arresting. They hired the architects
von Gerkan, Marg + Partner (GMP) to design a
structure with a sufficient span to allow two
747s and a smaller Airbus to be worked on
simultaneously. The resulting hangar is 150
metres (492 feet) long and 81 metres (266 feet)
deep, with a clear height of 23 metres (75 feet).
To create the clear span, two bow-arch trusses,
170 metres (558 feet) long and 30 metres (98
feet) high, were leant together over the roof, in
a method similar to the design of a suspension
bridge. With the cross-section of each bow arch
2 by 1.7 metres (6½ by 5½ feet), they weigh
2,800 tonnes, a load which is transferred to
buttresses on either side of the building. These
buttresses consist of H-shaped frames, between
which sit glazed boxes serving as storage areas
for the materials and hydraulic platforms used in
the servicing of the aircraft. The roof is made up
of an open grid structure of trusses, supported
by the arches via tension rods. The doors of the
hangar, 150 metres (492 feet) long and 22
metres (72 feet) high, are fully glazed, giving
passengers passing on taxiing aircraft a clear
view in. It is a rare case where the public are
given an insight into what is required to ensure
their safety.

The **New York Times Printing Works** by
Polshek and Partners, completed in 1997 in
Queens, New York, also gives passers-by – in this
case motorists – a glimpse of its contents.

HAMBURG MAINTENANCE HANGAR

RIGHT Two bow-arch trusses transfer the weight
to H-shaped frames that stand outside
the building envelope.

HAMBURG MAINTENANCE HANGAR

BELOW A space frame supported by the bow-
arches in turn supports lifting equipment.

NEW YORK TIMES PRINTING WORKS

ABOVE Literally a 'decorated shed'.

NEW YORK TIMES PRINTING WORKS

OPPOSITE Elements of the building are brightly
coloured in order to be seen from outside.

A simple industrial box, 50,166 square metres
(540,000 square feet) in size, it provides a literal
example of Robert Venturi's famous 'decorated
shed'. The logo of the paper has been added in
very large letters to the outside of the building,
and as a million motorists pass the factory each
week, this serves as a useful advert for the
newspaper. A glass window by the motorway
shows various aspects of the presses and the
papers passing through the building. This effect
is enhanced by a series of dramatic coloured
objects. Essentially this functions at the level
of bold graphics – there is nothing specifically
connecting the character of the building with
the character of the newspaper. Some buildings,
however, are consciously designed to present
their workings to the passer-by and also describe
the character of the company they house. These
retain the characteristics of the 'well-serviced

hangar', albeit one that is completely tailored to
the needs of a particular client.

The **Igus Factory**, near Cologne in Germany
(1990–92) by Nicholas Grimshaw and Partners
was one of the first industrial buildings designed
to accommodate the requirements of flexibility
idealized by Archigram and Cedric Price.
Grimshaw has utilized industrial commissions
in the development of his career and through
them he has devised systems of construction
which have then been employed on other
building types.

Günter Blasé, Chief Executive of Igus,
hand-picked Grimshaw because he felt that
Grimshaw's design principles would suit his own
corporate structure. Blasé owned a firm that
made injection-moulded plastics. A family
company also run by Günter's sons Frank and
Carsten, Igus employed a 'solar-system' model of

IGUS FACTORY

ABOVE Interchangeable cladding panels are either glazed or solid.

IGUS FACTORY

TOP RIGHT The masts are designed to be visible from the nearby motorway.

corporate structure that envisaged placing each client at the centre of 'the universe' with separate departments of the company answering directly to him. Blasé had visited various Grimshaw buildings and was attracted by Grimshaw's emphasis on flexibility. Certainly the factory was intended to be striking enough to raise the company's profile but it also had to accommodate future changes in its internal configuration. Thus Archigram's 'well-serviced shed' of neutral but equipped space was a fundamental practical requirement.

Grimshaw tackled this brief by devising a plan that would supply flexibility in two ways. First, it would provide large column-free spaces that would enable the factory's processes to be reorientated at a later date. Second, it would allow these spaces to accommodate interchangeable uses including offices for administrative staff and factory production facilities. In order to create an uninterrupted floor area, all the servicing requirements of the factory floor were either hung from the roof or run along first-floor walkways. These walkways also made it easy to oversee production on the factory floor below. The scheme was planned around an 11.25-metre (37-foot) square module. Four courtyards each contain a structural mast that supports a large square of building around it, creating a profile reminiscent of Powell & Moya's Skylon at the Festival of Britain in 1951. The masts are also tall enough to advertise the factory's presence to drivers on the nearby motorway. Inside the factory the masts allow clear spans of 33.75 metres (111 feet) in both directions. They do this by assisting in the support of a simple framework of 610-millimetre (24-inch) deep I-beam sections that directly hold up the roof. Each modular unit of the roof contains a 6-metre (20-foot) diameter prefabricated glass-reinforced plastic dome, which provides natural north light and ventilation while stopping any direct sunlight from reaching the factory floor. Administrative offices were placed on independently braced frames resembling 'legs' with flat disc-shaped 'feet'. These could be attached to the perimeter or could stand anywhere in the plan either alone or grouped together, deriving their natural light and ventilation from the roof modules.

IGUS FACTORY
PREVIOUS SPREAD Walkways allow supervision of production while leaving an uncluttered factory floor.

HACTL CARGO TERMINAL
LEFT The largest air cargo facility in the world.

HACTL CARGO TERMINAL
RIGHT Canyons are formed between the central Bulk Storage Systems (to the left) and peripheral Container Storage Systems (to the right).

that it has been lovingly detailed suggests that the same degree of care is applied to its products. While most beautifully crafted products evolve in very basic buildings, the Igus building suggests that its company's wares must be superior if the factory itself is so well made.

While specialized industries may provide the opportunity for architects to craft bespoke buildings, many large-scale industrial commissions already have the architect's limited role mapped out. Foster and Partners recently completed a gloriously expensive bespoke headquarters for Formula One constructors Maclaren. At the other end of the spectrum they have also designed the cargo terminal at Hong Kong Airport. The **HACTL Cargo Terminals** Ltd Superterminal 1 came into the office via the engineers Arup. Arup's relationship with HACTL dates back to 1983 when they were discovered in a telephone directory and asked to engineer an extension to Kai Tak's cargo facilities. They then built another new facility on the Kai Tak Airport site before being commissioned to build the largest air cargo facility in the world at Hong Kong's new airport of Chek Lap Kok.

The building basically contains storage racks for cargo and a complicated conveyor system for guiding individual containers to their appropriate rack. This is made more complex still by the fact that unlike heavy sea cargo containers, which are structurally very strong, lightweight air cargo containers need to be supported flat at all times. At the centre of the

The design of the prefabricated cladding allowed for standard panels, windows and doors to be interchangeable. The ribbed aluminium cladding is held to the vertical supports by anodized clamps. The combination of a number of uniquely designed and machined elements in the building gives it some of the characteristics of product design.

The Igus Factory has successfully served the company as an advert for flexibility. The fact

HACTL CARGO TERMINAL
PREVIOUS SPREAD Goods wait for processing outside the
HACTL cargo terminal.

HACTL CARGO TERMINAL
RIGHT Steel 'butterfly wing' trusses support the
Container Storage System (to the right).

building are two Bulk Storage Systems (BSS) and on the east and west façades two Container Storage Systems (CSS). In between are large flat warehouse floors where cargo is either packed into or unpacked from the containers. Unpacked cargo is then placed in steel mesh cages called 'bins' and taken to the BSS. Contained cargo is taken down from the accessible CSS and loaded onto aeroplanes. In between, it is unpacked and checked in the central Customs and Excise Hall. At the building's north end, next to the airport's apron, is a specialist perishable goods handling unit.

A separate Express Centre is housed in a separate building. This handles 200,000 tonnes of cargo per annum and has sorting facilities and offices for separate express cargo and courier operators. In addition there are office spaces and recreational facilities for the employees, but like the crew facilities of a container ship, these are of a secondary scale. Finally, the south façade administrative block contains offices for airlines, a 24-hour canteen over 3,500 square metres (37,700 square feet) and Chek Lap Kok's only HSBC bank. The workers also have open access to an enormous roof complete with tennis, basketball and five-a-side football courts and a swimming pool.

Foster and Partners designed the building on a very limited budget, but the essential processing diagrams which constitute the basis for the scheme are inherited from the client and the engineers. The CSS wings were built as separate stand-alone steel structures in order to keep their construction schedule wholly independent of the concrete structure of the main building. The efficiency of an air cargo facility is determined by the length of building accessible from the air side. By pulling the CSSs 16 metres (52 feet) away from the main structure the design added two additional interfaces per CSS, making six in total. The building therefore has a colossal two kilometres (1¼ miles) of interface length. It also allows far greater access for fire vehicles. Steel 'butterfly wing' trusses support the roof of the roadway and are lined with louvers that encourage natural ventilation while protecting the corridor from the sun. While the long exterior façades of the CSS are glazed they are open at low level, which serves to draw air in through the CSS.

The HACTL Cargo Terminal shows that the technical requirements of buildings that are not primarily for human habitation often place constraints on the programmatic pretensions of architects. Foster and Partners were approached by their engineering partner Arup because they would be amenable to accepting that the essential diagram of the building had already been established and prepared to design those visual elements that could express that diagram clearly. The design of modern industrial buildings can thus present the architect with limited options. Foster and Partners were able to concentrate their focus on what could be achieved. The phrase 'functionalism' has been so tainted by its misappropriation in the service of the early generations of Modern Movement architecture that it now has little clear meaning. But these industrial buildings are clearly far more directly 'functional' in the sense of reflecting a functional brief in a much less rhetorical way than those of the early modernists. They are successful because they are only in a limited sense 'designed', providing neutral spaces within which industrial practice can change.

As a consequence these large-volume buildings are also easily adapted to alternative uses. To some extent this facility has been consciously sought but it is also indicates just how quixotic technology and economics can be. While Cargolifter now houses a tropical island holiday park, Grimshaw's famous Financial Times Printing Works provides office space for a computer company. Whether their architects rejoiced as this seminal principle of Buckminster Fuller and Archigram was implemented isn't recorded.

TRANSPORT

TRANSPORT
People Processors

PREVIOUS SPREAD Inchon Transportation Centre
(Terry Farrell & Partners)

During the 19th century the most ubiquitous sign of the Industrial Revolution was the spread of the railway network across the countryside of western Europe. It represented what people then described as the forces of the 'New Age'. Some artists found the advent of the railways inspiring. One of J. M. W. Turner's later masterpieces, *Rain, Steam and Speed – the Great Western Railway* (1844) was a reaction to the railway mania that gripped England in the 1840s. An exhilarating image, it clearly proclaimed that a train crossing the Brunel-designed Maidenhead Bridge was a thing of great beauty. Claude Monet painted the new St-Lazare railway station no fewer than eight times. Many others, including the novelist Thomas Hardy, saw the railway as a malignant presence, the destroyer of rural life. But whether for good or ill, its importance as a social catalyst was recognized immediately.

Railway stations became some of the most influential products of 19th-century engineering. Isambard Kingdom Brunel, the visionary engineer behind the Great Western Railway, completed Paddington Station in 1851. With a central span of 31 metres (102 feet) and side aisles of 21 metres (69 feet), it heralded a new scale of architecture in iron. In 1868 Paddington was dwarfed by the 73-metre (240-foot) span of St Pancras Station, which in 1893 was itself overtaken by the 98-metre (322-foot) span of Philadelphia's Broad Street Station.

The high spanning arches of 19th-century railway termini were designed both to protect passengers from the rain and to accommodate the smoke that billowed out of the steam engines. When diesel and electric power replaced steam, railway stations were generally built with cheaper, more modest, concrete structures. Yet the symbolic attraction of the large-span arch remained. The universal acclaim that greeted the original Eurostar terminal completed in 1993 at Waterloo by Nicholas Grimshaw and Partners owed much to its retention of this ideal, though here it took a striking curved form. Indeed, Grimshaw himself described it in an interview on the BBC as 'a train hall in the real heroic tradition of Victorian railway stations.'[1]

In 2000 Foster and Partners built a station that reinterpreted the gateway arch but for the needs of a different climate. **Expo Station** is located on the Changi Airport Mass Rapid Transit (MRT) Line connecting Changi Airport to the centre of Singapore. Despite being a relatively small provincial station, its 70-metre (230-foot) span, is still comparable with that of St Pancras. While its oversailing roof indicates how little station designs have changed, the shape of that roof indicates what has. Expo Station is curved in three directions in a 130-metre (427-foot) long torus, made possible by the use of a 'diagrid' of steel members. The resulting form is lifted onto only four pairs of V-shaped twin columns. Because the trains are air-conditioned, the station has simply to provide a canopy in the tropical climate. This is clad in titanium to deflect the heat of the sun, and its shape helps create a microclimate that keeps the temperature on the platforms up to four degrees

EXPO STATION
ABOVE The curved train shed is reinterpreted as a torus on four legs with a separate circular disk.

EXPO STATION
OPPOSITE The soffit reflects light onto the station platforms.

OLYMPIC PARK RAILWAY

RIGHT Gaps above the centre of each column
provide a visual lightness where one
might expect visual weight.

OLYMPIC PARK RAILWAY

FOLLOWING SPREAD The thin steel folded vault resembles
a giant work of origami.

lower than 'outside'. At the same time the underside of the structure is covered in mirrored stainless steel in order to reflect light in.

The Expo Station is designed to act as the landmark for the Expo site and, as such, the shape of the building reflects a self-conscious futurism. The ticket hall, for instance, is protected from the rain by a cantilevered stainless steel disc 38 metres (125 feet) in diameter, and has a striking circular lift set below it. Like its 19th-century predecessors, the Expo Station is a symbolic as well as a practical building, and part of that symbolism is the projection of an association between the Expo site and the future, or at least the technological limits of today.

The **Olympic Park Railway** at Homebush Bay shows a similar desire to celebrate the entrance to its site, and acted as the literal gateway to the Sydney Olympics. Designed by Rodney Uren and Ken Maher of architects Hassell, this building serves as both a visible civic landmark and an underground station handling up to 50,000 people per hour. While the platforms sit at 6.5 metres (21 feet) below ground level, the land above has been excavated, and then topped with a striking steel structure, visible from around the site. This 200-metre (656-foot) open-ended canopy is clad in zincalume-coated steel decking, and is entirely services free. It is supported by eighteen pairs of Vierendeel steel trusses that straddle 11-metre (35-foot) high pre-cast concrete columns.

Gaps are left above the centre of each column between the roof bays, giving a visual lightness at the point of expectation of visual weight. The thin steel folded vault resembles a giant work of origami – curiously evocative of the light card models made by the architects in the course of its design. One bizarre by-product of the futuristic projection of both stations is an organic imagery. In the case of the Expo Station this takes the form of a four-legged beetle and at Homebush a multi-legged caterpillar.

Rail transport has recently received fresh impetus through the construction of new high-speed techniques for international travel. But this only applies to areas of the world with dense populations such as Asia and Europe where rail can compete with air travel. For during the course of the 20th century, airports quickly emerged as the most important transport interchanges on the planet. Today, airports are arguably the world's most important and expensive building type. They are also of enormous strategic significance, and tend to be the first complexes seized during a revolution or coup d'état.

The airport is also one of the few new typologies to date from the modernist period of architectural history. Early on its growth was recognized as a visible symbol of the zeitgeist and airports were popular with the first generation of modernists. The early modernist airport projects displayed the same concerns with 'total design' evident in other building

forms. For a long time architects couldn't resist the seductive idea of planes taking off from the flat roofs of their buildings. In 1914 Antonio Sant'Elia had this idea, and it was retained by Le Corbusier in his 1922 Ville Contemporaine. As Hugh Pearman, author of *Airports: A century of architecture* complains, 'this shows a complete ignorance of the ground-hugging, land-hungry nature of real airports, which even then was becoming apparent.'[2] Airports require space for a whole range of hangar, maintenance and administration buildings, as well as terminals. The direction of the wind affects the direction of take-off and a rooftop design would never allow for changes in plane type, which might require longer runways.

Like the great engineering projects of the 19th century, an airport project brief has a very different character to that of other building types. Architects do not design them from scratch. Passenger terminals are instead devised as part of vast infrastructure projects. First, a strategy is formulated, then tested, and then finally the diagram for a terminal agreed upon. While this is open to further formulation, to some extent this diagram has to form the basis of the design. As a consequence, architects accustomed to determining the spatial arrangement of their buildings would find the design of an airport very difficult. They may only be able to manipulate the section of a structure whose plan is fixed, and even then they will be expected to find highly efficient solutions

hand-in-hand with engineers. To some extent
this caution is due to the complexity of the
building type; it also reflects the degree of
scrutiny applied to projects whose cost is
measured in billions of dollars.

Architects whose interests lie in
diagrammatic solutions developed in close
collaboration with engineers are obviously well
placed to provide the sorts of practical solutions
that airport planners are looking for. As a
consequence 'problem-solvers' have been
commissioned to build many of the most
prestigious projects. Norman Foster, for
example, began with the new London airport,
Stansted (1986–91), and moved on to the largest
and most ambitious airport projects constructed
to date, first at Hong Kong's Chek Lap Kok
(1992–8), and currently at Beijing. Richard
Rogers has had to labour through the planning
tedium involved in the construction of London
Heathrow's Terminal 5 and, in the course of this
project, has built a much larger terminal at
Barajas in Madrid (2001–2006). Renzo Piano has
gone on to design an enormous new airport at
Kansai (1988–94) and Kisho Kurokawa has done
the same at Kuala Lumpur International Airport
(1993–8). Nicholas Grimshaw has built an Airside
Centre at Zurich (2004), while even Terry Farrell
has returned to his engineered-aesthetic roots to
build the transportation centre at Inchon in
South Korea (1996–2002). The careers of
Meinhard von Gerkan and Volkwin Marg (GMP)
are virtually the product of an airport design,

winning an international competition for Berlin-
Tegel airport in 1965, a year after leaving college.

The design of a passenger terminal involves
two different types of building with separate
functions. The first contains the departures and
arrivals halls where passengers and their luggage
are processed. These tend to have big deep plans.
The second are the gates, which act as holding
bays and embarkation pens. These tend to be
thin linear structures.

In the late 1980s oversailing steel roofs
carried on large spans became the dominant
visual feature of airport design, replacing the
range of concrete solutions popular in the 1960s
and 1970s. These were not just adopted in the
larger airport schemes but became the defining
feature of smaller ones as well. The big roof had
advantages both as a form of orientation, and
also as an opportunity to offer visual clarity
above an ever-expanding morass of retail outlets
and security partitions at ground level. Foster
and Partners' Stansted Airport in London
established a lightweight series of modular
domes supported by distinctive 'Y'-shaped
columns. The roof carries no servicing, which is
instead located in the columns. At night its white
canopy serves as a huge light reflector.

Von Gerkan Marg + Partner (GMP), in
collaboration with Karsten Brauer, built
something similar at **Stuttgart Airport** in 1991.
Here the columns were made into more
complex and explicitly tree-like structures, while
the roof itself was not entirely services free.

It succeeded in one way that Stansted failed, by using a stepped section banking up towards airside. A continuous flat roof followed this sloped profile and gave a very clear sense of orientation to the passenger, as well as allowing the visitor finally to walk outside at the uppermost restaurant level and enjoy a viewing platform over the aeroplanes below. The problem with Stansted was that its perfect Euclidian geometry made everything in every direction look identical and it was thus necessary to use the much-despised mess of retail units and security barriers at ground level as guides.

At the later Terminal 3 at Stuttgart, GMP used the same idea with the added subtlety that the airside slope was split into three separate soffits with light penetrating

between them. Both terminals have tree-like
supports, which start with a central column but
split into forty-eight members on their way to
the ceiling. In the vertical breaks of Terminal 3,
however, each layer is supported by a separate
row of 'trees' giving an even clearer sense of a
kind of metal forest canopy.

GMP used a slightly different system at
Hamburg Airport in 1994. As at Stuttgart, the
building's section climbs towards airside, with
retail concessions kept above the check-in and
security level on galleries that look back towards
landside. At Hamburg the columns are simplified
to support long curved trusses, which in turn
support the roof purlins. These are reminiscent
of the wooden frameworks of early aircraft
designs, a rich source of imagery that often

recurs in terminal design. The large-span roof
of the departure hall is sandwiched by two
office buildings with independent frames.
These buildings abut awkwardly, though
they allow the office workers to use the same
landside facilities as departing passengers.

Clear metaphors used at Stuttgart and
Hamburg – trees and aircraft – give a distinct
personality to these otherwise anonymous
large-volume spaces, countering the tendency
of international airports to appear
indistinguishable from one another, particularly
when jet-lagged. **Oslo's Gardermoen Airport**,
designed by the consortium Aviaplan AS in 1995
with architect Niels Torp, also illustrates how the
large-volume terminal building does not have to
be overpowering or anonymous. It was initially

HAMBURG AIRPORT

PREVIOUS SPREAD Curved trusses evoke the wooden
frameworks of early aircraft.

HAMBURG AIRPORT

OPPOSITE Looking towards airside from check-in.

HAMBURG AIRPORT

BELOW The terminal is awkwardly 'bookended'
by two blocks of offices.

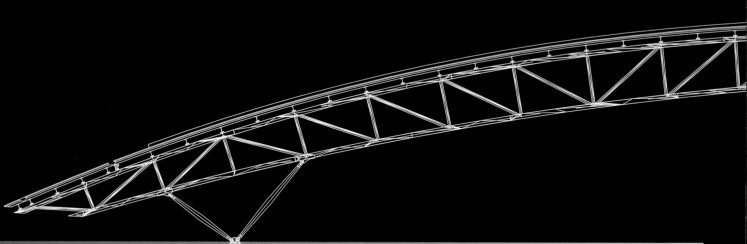

OSLO GARDERMOEN AIRPORT

OPPOSITE Airside showing extruding ends
of glue-laminated beams.

OSLO GARDERMOEN AIRPORT

ABOVE An underground tunnel connects
the current terminal to a site on the
other side of the runway, allowing
for future expansion.

LEFT The airport has limited the number of
concessions in order to maintain a sleek,
uncluttered interior.

designed with a steel roof, but after political
pressure was built with Norwegian wooden
glue-laminated beams. The products of the
Norwegian timber industry also clad the
interior, along with Norwegian slate. Offices are
held in three pods that stand within the larger
terminal space, and have curved walls clad in
glass and wood. At the same time the signage of
retail outlets is suppressed. The result is an
interior with a very clear national identity. Built
on an old military base, Gardermoen has been
planned for future expansion. Tunnels built
under the runway will minimize disruption
during further phases of construction. The
terminal is also one of the first to have its
temperature controlled through thermal storage
using groundwater. It therefore anticipates the
temperature differential of the Scandinavian
climate and reduces the huge energy
requirements common to buildings of this size.

Individual passenger terminals first reached
a scale measurable in kilometres rather than
metres in Asia. Here air travel has expanded
faster than in anywhere else in the world.
A series of enormous buildings have been built
on greenfield sites. All were initiated before the
Asian crash of the late 1990s, and all reflect civic
pride and ambition as well as responding to a
predicted growth in passenger numbers. In Hong
Kong, Osaka and Seoul this has necessitated
building out into the sea to satisfy the airports'
massive requirements for flat land. During
construction at Kansai the number of people

OSLO GARDERMOEN AIRPORT

OPPOSITE Giant glue-laminated beams are
supported by concrete columns.

OSLO GARDERMOEN AIRPORT

BELOW AND Arrivals gate – the building is rich
FOLLOWING SPREAD in Norwegian materials such as slate
and softwoods.

KANSAI AIRPORT
RIGHT The product of Japan's first international
architecture competition.

KANSAI AIRPORT
FOLLOWING SPREAD A lattice structure of arched trusses
formed of 244 steel ribs makes up the
1.5-kilometre (one-mile) curve.

working on site peaked at 10,000, whereas this figure climbed to 21,000 at Hong Kong. In both cases this meant ferrying out the entire workforce every day.

Kansai Airport in Japan, the first of these new international hubs, was built between 1988 and 1994. The Kansai region has twenty million inhabitants, two large industrial cities, Osaka and Kobe, and two cultural centres, Kyoto and Nara. It is a region that has lately fallen well behind Tokyo economically — indeed Tokyo's port, Yokohama, has overtaken Osaka as Japan's second city.

Osaka's existing airport, Itami, had become hemmed in by buildings and could not offer growth of a sufficient scale to sustain the region's economy. As a result it was decided to build a new airport 5 kilometres (3 miles) offshore on an artificial island in Osaka Bay, 40 kilometres (25 miles) south-west of the city centre. The great advantage of this decision was that Kansai could become Japan's first airport to operate 24 hours a day, providing a capacity of 160,000 flights and 25 million passengers a year.

Three mountains had to be demolished to make up the 511-hectare (1,260-acre) artificial island, now one of the few man-made objects visible from space. Initially six huge Japanese design/construction companies were asked to submit designs for the passenger terminal. The chosen scheme, by Nikken Sekkei, was then distributed to a number of international consultancies for comment. Of these, Paul Andreu of Aéroports de Paris, returned an entirely new proposal: a single building that combined the functions of international and domestic services on different levels and enabled fast connections between the two. Andreu envisaged this as a single long linear terminal matching the linear island, one which would encourage the planning of efficient taxiways and provide passengers with fast access to the planes.

During the 1980s the closed character of the Japanese market had become the subject of complaints, especially from the United States and it was therefore decided to hold Japan's first international competition to determine the lead designers. Renzo Piano was one of the architects asked to enter. By 1988 he had built up a very large and successful practice, the Renzo Piano Building Workshop (RPBW), but since he had had no previous experience in airport design he was reluctant to commit the necessary man-hours to enter a competition he was unlikely to win. Piano, however, had two Japanese associates Noriaki Okabe and Shunji Ishida, who were keen to enter the competition. They approached the engineer Peter Rice of Ove Arup, and Rice persuaded Piano.

RPBW alone among the competition entrants retained Paul Andreu's diagram in which domestic flights docked on the central section of the building, while international flights used the wings on either side. Therefore, when RPBW won it ensured that Kansai would become synonymous with a long linear shape. Rather than delegate construction to a Japanese partner, as the competition organizers had assumed, Piano immediately set up a consortium that included RPBW, Nikken Sekkei, Aéroports de Paris and Japan Airports Consultants. Piano accepted that Nikken Sekkei should be given the practical lower floors to detail and construct. As a result RPBW's steel and glass structure sits on top of a Nikken Sekkei inner building with a traditional heavy concrete frame. RPBW have made the relationship between the two very explicit. The footings of the roof's great trusses appear to flare out to meet the concrete slab below. But the flare shape is actually just a cover that fireproofs the real structure whose loads are, in fact, transferred to columns passing through the slab. The Nikken Sekkei building has thus been treated as the topography on which RPBW's sinuous steel form sits.

Kansai's extraordinary shape is the product of rather abstract reasoning. First, RPBW drew a huge torus with a radius of 16.4 kilometres (10 miles). This was then placed at an angle to the plane of the ground that left most of it hidden below the surface of the earth. Left above ground was a gentle curve, tipped over towards the airside and reaching its apex at the centre. This would become the shape of the building, and the result was a complex but geometrically accurate three-dimensional curved form. The advantage of using a strict geometry was that

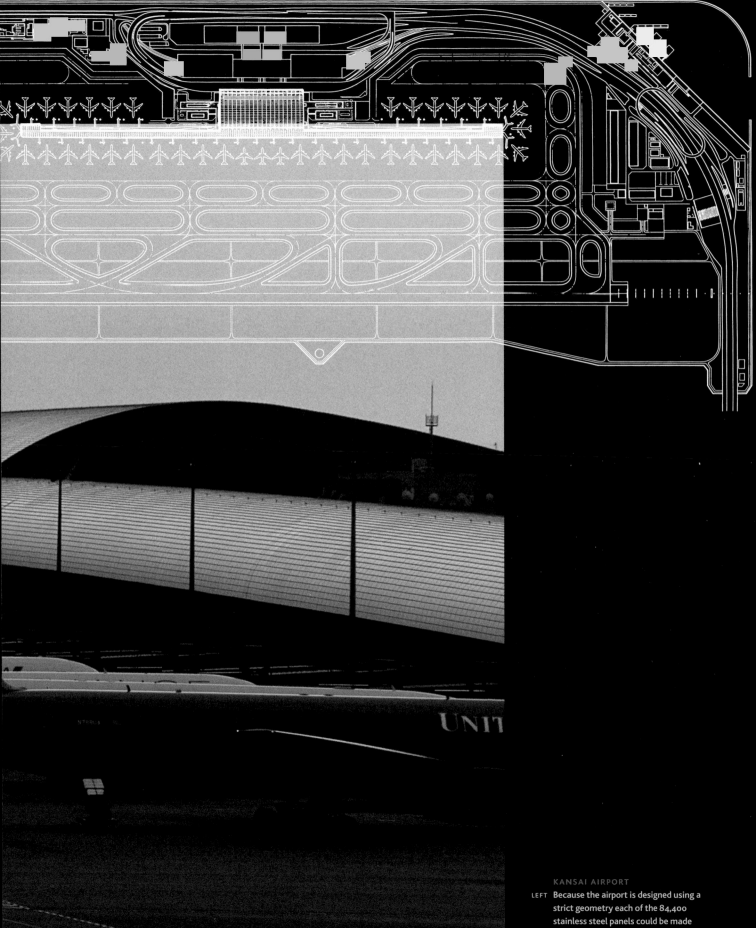

KANSAI AIRPORT

RIGHT The 'canyon' designed to get people
to the right level.

KANSAI AIRPORT

LEFT A single departure lounge runs the
entire length of the building.

the 84,400 stainless steel panels that cover the roof could all be made exactly the same size. These were small enough (1.8 by 0.6 metres – 6 by 2 feet) to both match the curvature of the 90,000 square metre (970,000 square foot) roof and to be carried around by one person. They were also durable enough to withstand the corrosive saltwater environment and, with a hairline finish, dull enough not to dazzle pilots or air traffic control. They protected a second layer below, which provided waterproofing and insulation.

The shape is maintained by a lattice structure of arched trusses, and supported by 244 steel ribs set at 7.2-metre (24-foot) intervals that gradually reduce in length as the structure shrinks towards the wings. These ribs are connected to the lower level of the building with pin-joints. The secondary structure, which runs both the length of the building and diagonally behind the ribs, is made of square section steel tubing. Diaphragms made of steel tension rods at two-bay (14.4-metre/48-foot) intervals hold the whole thing together. Expansion joints, 450–600 millimetres (17–24 inches) wide, are placed in eleven locations at 150-metre (492-foot) intervals along the building's length. This results in layers of visible structure that Renzo Piano likened to 'an aircraft fuselage with the skin peeled off to let in light and give a glimpse of the underlying construction.'[3] The disadvantage is that it leaves the soffit looking incredibly 'busy', weakening the visual impact.

KANSAI AIRPORT

ABOVE AND OPPOSITE The departure hall contains Teflon scoops that entrain air below the soffit.

Another potential problem with the absence of a suspended ceiling was that it would leave the air-conditioning system very visible. In response, Tom Barker, the Arup services engineer, proposed blowing a jet of air from the landside across to the airside and then entraining it against the ceiling. The profile of the ceiling would then follow the natural curve of the decelerating air. This determined the curve of the airside façade, and made the shape more directional as the curve it produced tightened progressively.

RPBW ensured clear orientation within the terminal by moving all the major concessions – shops and restaurants – to a separate level between departures and arrivals. This left the sight lines for these levels as clear as possible, and also sandwiched the concessions between two concrete slabs so, if necessary, they could be sealed off behind fire doors and doused by sprinkler systems.

The scheme's only problem with orientation lies on the landside. Originally a huge glass wall was designed to greet visitors arriving by train and the layout of departures/arrivals would be visible behind this wall across an open 'canyon'. Unfortunately financial cutbacks forced the replacement of glass with a solid wall, and the view has been further obscured by the structure of the road. As a result, passengers tend to walk past the escalators, which operate just within the doorway, and then have to double back when they realize they are at the wrong level. The canyon's second problem is its colour scheme, where soft, almost pastel, colours were chosen to echo those of traditional Japanese architecture. However, today these colours are more reminiscent of Japanese toys (like the

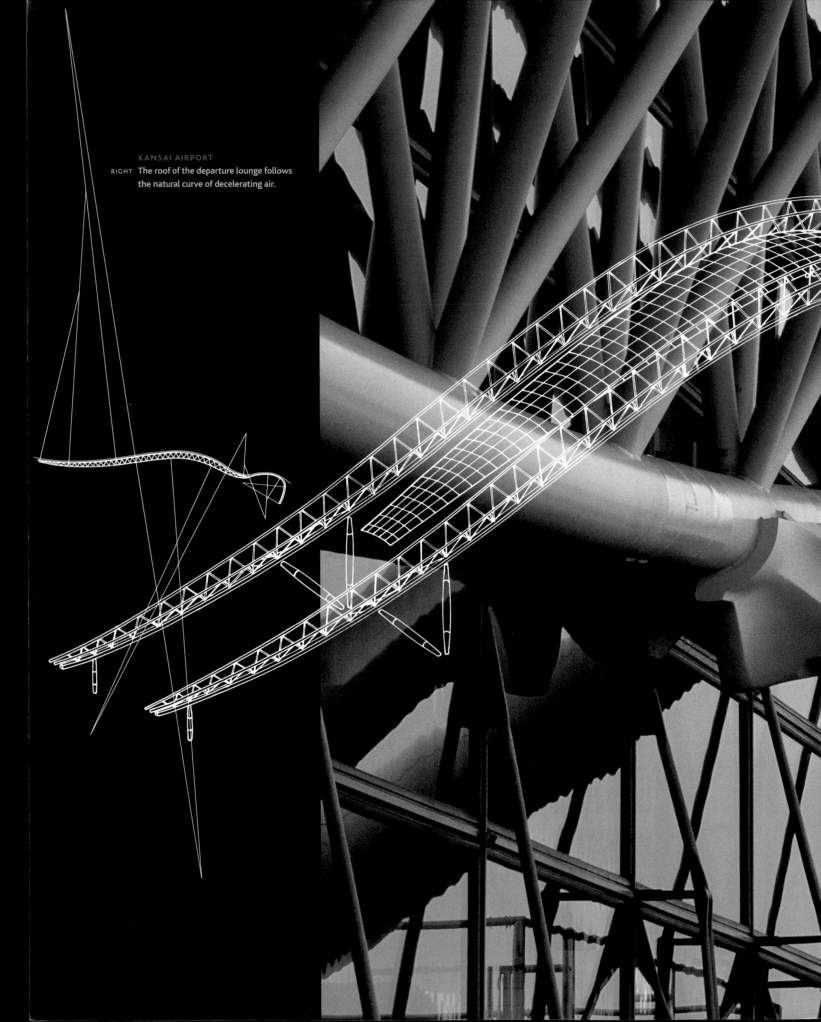

KANSAI AIRPORT
RIGHT The roof of the departure lounge follows
the natural curve of decelerating air.

ubiquitous 'Hello Kitty') than traditional Japanese architecture. Nor do they match the sleek grey engineered-aesthetic of the rest of the building.

Kansai takes the form of a single grand gesture that aims to evoke the majesty of air transport. The 1.7-kilometre (one-mile) long room could have felt like a never-ending tunnel, but because it curves in both directions it gives the viewer the sense of a controlled coherent space. Outside, it looks particularly dramatic counterpoised by the utter flatness of the artificial island and the greater flatness of the sea. The airport does not have to compete with even distant landforms and on a foggy day both Osaka and even the causeway disappear from view. This was also a shape to inspire a competition jury in which the presentation of a compelling model would be crucial – like the finished building, the model would be viewed from the air.

In Hong Kong the decision to build an airport at **Chek Lap Kok** was taken during a delicate political period. This British colony was about to be handed back to China, and its economic future was far from guaranteed. It had served very successfully as an economic bridge

between China and the West, but just as it was being returned to Chinese rule, China was itself opening up to trade with the outside world. On a strategic level Shanghai and Beijing would offer alternative sites for Asian headquarters, while at a regional level, the cities of the Pearl River Basin offered alternative sites for regional business. Hong Kong's existing airport, Kai Tak, whose runway extended into Hong Kong's harbour, was acting at capacity, and was already the third busiest in the world with 35 million passengers each year. Existing airports at Shenzhen and Guangzhou might be expanded to service the massive expansion of traffic predicted to accompany the growth of China's economy. Already half the world's population lay within five hours' flight of Hong Kong.

The outgoing British administration decided to develop a new airport site with potential for expansion. Given the shortage of flat land, the small island of Chek Lap Kok to the north of Lantau Island was chosen. It would be connected to the rest of Hong Kong by new transport links. The result was a massive infrastructure project called the 'Airport Core Programme', which included, along with the new airport, two new suspension bridges, a new

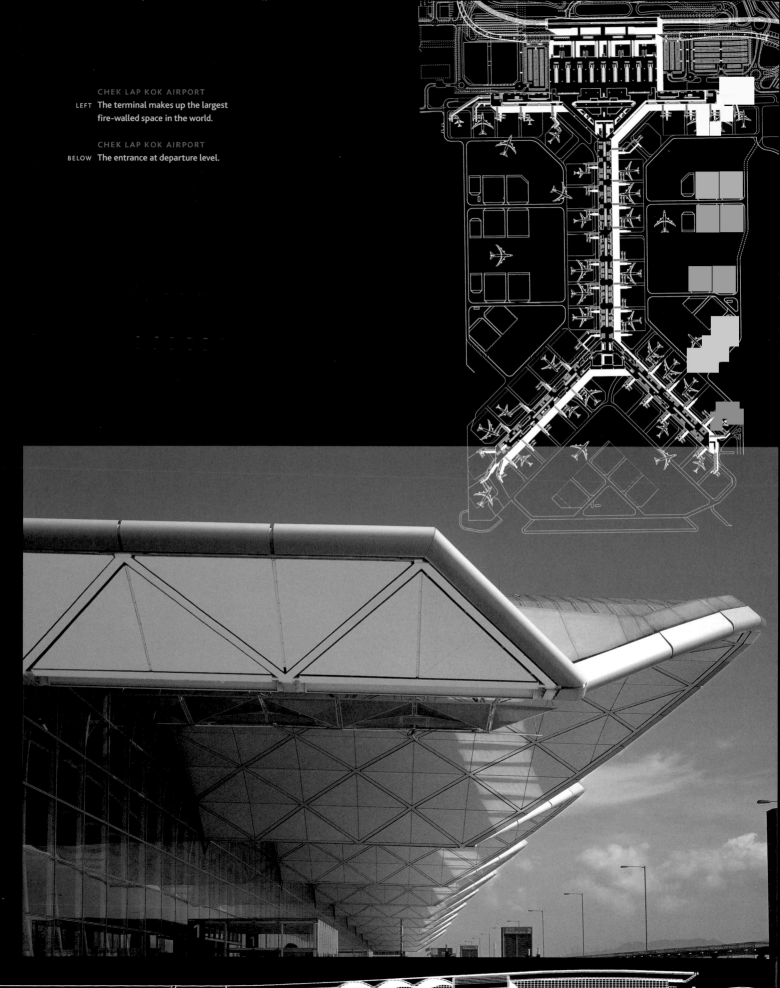

CHEK LAP KOK AIRPORT
LEFT The terminal makes up the largest fire-walled space in the world.

CHEK LAP KOK AIRPORT
BELOW The entrance at departure level.

six-lane motorway, a new tunnel under Hong
Kong's harbour and a new town for 20,000
residents called Tung Chung.

Chep Lap Kok island was flattened to
a uniform height of 6 metres (21 feet) and
augmented with reclaimed land to create a
1,255-hectare (3,100-acre) platform at a cost
of HK$9 billion. The original masterplan brief
was prepared by two consultants – Griener
International Ltd and Maunsell Consultants –
and put out to tender. At this point, the airport's
distinctive 'Y'-shaped plan servicing forty-eight
aircraft gates, a key characteristic of the finished
terminal, had already been determined. The
competition was won by the Mott Consortium,
a partnership of Mott Connell Ltd, Foster and
Partners and the British Airport Authority plc.
Ove Arup and Partners were then appointed to
prepare the scheme design of the superstructure
and all the visible steelwork.

The result is a terminal building with a
footprint twice the size of Kansai Airport. It is
1.27 kilometres (1 mile) long, with a gross floor
area of 516,000 square metres (5,550,000 square
feet). Arrivals, departures and baggage-handling
are each assigned a separate level. Passengers
arrive and proceed all the way through the
building to the train link to the city on the same
level. Departing passengers change levels only
once and do so via gentle 1:20 ramps.

The building was planned on a 36-metre
(120-foot) square module, and the module
neatly accommodates a single check-in counter

RIGHT This view of the baggage hall indicates
the monumental scale of the airport's
lower level.

and a single baggage handling unit. The columns
on the upper floors of the main processing
building are also set on a 36-metre (120-foot)
grid. While the majority of the terminal is made
of concrete, the roof, which gives Chek Lap Kok
its visual identity, is a lightweight steel structure
that follows the tradition of so many buildings
from Foster and Partners. It covers more than
18 hectares (45 acres) and was prefabricated in
modules welded together on site. There are 129
in total and each fits a 36-metre square of the
grid. Each weighs between 100 and 150 tonnes,
(giving a weight per span of 54 kilos per square
metre – 11 pounds per square foot) and they are
made of a diagonal lattice of standard 406-
millimetre (16-inch) deep I-beams. Together the
roof modules make up a multi-barrel vault
structure. These vaults are aligned parallel to the
direction of passenger flow and therefore, unlike
Stansted, assist in orientation. The height of
the roof rises over the big public spaces of
departures and, at the far end of the building
spine, the West Hall. It drops down over the
linear spine and wings. As the 36-metre (120-
foot) column grid in the departures hall is
reduced to 18 metres (59 feet) in the linear spine
and wings, it became possible to omit the ties
across the vaults where they come closer to
people's heads. While the vaults are free from
mechanical services, at the apex of each one a
gantry hangs below a skylight reflecting light
up and across the roof. Its triangular pattern
continues the structural ribs of the vault's arch.

INCHON TRANSPORTATION CENTRE
LEFT The central tube will contain a train link.

INCHON TRANSPORTATION CENTRE
OPPOSITE Seen from the airport the building has a
self-conscious futurism.

INCHON TRANSPORTATION CENTRE
FOLLOWING Farrell understood that this central space,
SPREAD with its 180-metre (590-foot) span, would
serve as the visual focus of the airport.

for a building of this size, it has the potential to
expand to a capacity of 80 million, making it a
serious global competitor. Indeed, Chep Lap Kok
is now the world's largest airport, with the
biggest passenger terminal, cargo terminal and
in-flight catering operation.

Inchon Airport, which serves Korea's capital
Seoul, shares many of the characteristics of
Kansai and Chek Lap Kok. It is intended to serve
as an international as well as a regional hub,
and was largely built on reclaimed land – in this
case between two islands, Yong Jong and Yong
Yu. It was also part of a massive infrastructural
project including the construction of an eight-
lane motorway, a new train link, an underwater
road tunnel, a high-speed ferry service and
new helicopter routes. The framework into
which this fits was determined by an airport
consultant, Bechtel of San Francisco, whose
client was the Korean Airport Construction
Authority (KOACA).

The design of Inchon Airport began in 1992
with an invited competition for a curved
terminal building. It was won by Fentress
Bradburn of Denver, USA, in collaboration with
Korean Architects Collaborative International.
They followed Bechtel's plan for a crescent-
shaped terminal with two outstretched arms, at
the apex of which would be a separate
Transportation Centre. This centre is the airport's
real grand gesture, the most visually dominant
and iconic aspect of the scheme. It serves as the
focus of the symmetrical plan where railway

Longitudinally the roof includes three
movement joints but across the vaults there are
none as each vault is itself designed to flex.

The whole roof encloses the largest fire-
walled space in the world. Supported by
bowstring trusses, the glass walls of the terminal
rise to a height of 21 metres (69 feet) and have
been engineered to withstand the wind loads of
Hong Kong's regular typhoons.

The passenger terminal at Chek Lap Kok,
with its generous proportions, provides a real
sense of drama. The great gates, huge West Hall
and long spinal corridor climax in the massive
'meeting and greeting' hall, one of Hong Kong's
rare large public spaces. The drama is continued
in the series of vistas seen from the train as it
makes its way into the city. While the current
capacity of 35 million passengers a year is small

INCHON TRANSPORTATION CENTRE

LEFT Originally the trusses were designed to be
entirely hidden by a false ceiling, like that
of a Baroque church.

INCHON TRANSPORTATION CENTRE

FOLLOWING The Transportation Centre sits at the
SPREAD centre of the curved airport complex.
It takes the engineered-aesthetic to its
logical conclusion: science fiction.

lines travelling along an axis reach the terminal
splayed out beyond them. Following a separate
competition the **Transportation Centre** was
awarded to Terry Farrell & Partners. Their
competition scheme showed a clear grasp of
the required sense of drama. The brief was for a
building to provide access to three rail networks,
to buses and coaches, taxi and car rental and
three below-ground levels of parking. Originally
it included an air traffic control tower as well.
Farrell's scheme made the traffic control tower
an integral element – the 'head' of an organic
form resembling a long-necked bird.

The brief was later adjusted and the
control tower moved, but the 'head' shape
remains and its present function is to assist in
the ventilation of the massive room below. Like
the 'bird in flight', which the building is proposed
to resemble, the room is described as the 'Great
Hall', a name derived from traditional Korean
architecture. Now higher than the competition
entry, its sculptural shape suggests that the
building does much more than simply provide
access to the various elevators and entrances.
The 'front' (north) façade that faces airside has
a concave curved wall reflecting the curve of
the walkway, which connects it to the terminal.
On either side of the Great Hall two wings
spread out covering the train platforms.

Terry Farrell & Partners appear less
concerned with structural clarity, in the High-
Tech sense, than RPBW or Foster. The structure
is welded in the Asian tradition rather than

INCHON TRANSPORTATION CENTRE
OPPOSITE Trusses are welded rather than pin-jointed
in the High-Tech tradition.

mechanically jointed. A series of arched trusses span up to 180 metres (590 feet). Most of them do not reach the ground but transfer their loads to other trusses that arch over the side walls. Consequently, the roof seems to sit on two large piers in the corners of the hall and on a solid wall at the back. Originally all the trusses would have been clad inside had it not been for a client request that left those under the rooflight exposed. Otherwise they are covered in perforated panels. In fact Terry Farrell & Partners originally wanted to create wholly separate interior and exterior forms, like the domes of Baroque architecture. As it is, a substantial unseen volume of structure remains between the two roofs inside and out.

Nonetheless, Farrell has been keen to stress the building's technological credentials. Its form was modelled with a CATIA program used by aeroplane designers, albeit following contours first modelled by hand. As Farrell explains: 'I've always been interested in technology, which was a big issue at Inchon...the construction of the curving form was akin to automobile design.'[4] Certainly Farrell, when in partnership with Nicholas Grimshaw, was involved in what became described as 'High-Tech'. But subsequently he became one of the best-known and most successful architects to use a post-modernist vocabulary full of exaggerated classical motifs.

Farrell is quoted as seeing some relationship between his post-modern projects and Inchon in terms of an approach to urbanism. 'Urban design meets architecture in Inchon...and projects like Charing Cross Station and Blackfriars Bridge Station use the same language.' But here the language he has adopted involves a huge organically shaped lightweight steel structure. With its space pod 'docked' on the roof, Farrell's building is more an evocation of a UFO landing in the wilderness than something inspired by any pre-existing urban context. Its iconography suggests that the building appears as it does in order to satisfy some complex functional requirements.

If the dominant aesthetic in airport design has become the technological hangar, Farrell's Inchon searches for the visual techno-edge, as can be seen in some of the overtly space-tech interior surfaces. Some columns have tapered cladding and curved vertical fins attached to the exterior pedestrian bridges, and at night the space-pod has coloured lights. Farrell, who is prepared to go to more rhetorical lengths than his erstwhile 'High-Tech' colleagues, looks to take the engineered-aesthetic to its logical conclusion: science fiction.

The iconic function of this building was appreciated when, after the 1997 Asian financial crash, it was financed directly by the Korean government after no commercial source of finance could be found. It was thus complete for Korea's co-hosting of the 2002 World Cup. Without Inchon, Korea's gateway project would have looked much less impressive even if it had worked just as well.

The large-span engineered-aesthetic solution has been imported into Asia to express an overwhelming sense of grandeur, of arrival and hence of the importance of the host city. These buildings are very expensive civic symbols as well as airports. At present Singapore's Changi Airport handles more passengers per year than any of them, but consists of a series of low spaces designed by local architects. It is a very efficient airport to arrive at and passengers can travel from the plane to the city far quicker than in any of these illustrious examples. However, it fails to provide any sense of civic drama. For that, a large-volume structure is required.

There are, however, potential problems in all this expansion. First were the technical problems inevitable with projects of this ambition. At Chek Lap Kok much of the glass of the terminal building had to be replaced, and Kansai's island initially threatened to sink into the sea. But the lasting problems are strategic. These airports directly compete for air traffic. Kansai Airport is currently expanding but is laden with debt. The arrival of Inchon has also provided it with a serious competitor as many travellers to Japan change planes there from international flights to provincial Japanese airports. More broadly there is no guarantee that numbers will increase to the levels predicted, particularly as all these schemes were initiated before the Asian financial crash of the late 1990s.

In Europe the same intense international
competition is affecting the largest airports.
The most ambitious recent European airport
terminal building was opened in 2006 at **Barajas
Airport**, Madrid. While its existing overcrowded
terminals are already Europe's fifth busiest, the
new terminal is intended to allow Barajas to
compete with Frankfurt, Charles de Galle and
Heathrow by doubling its capacity to 70 million
a year. This reflects Madrid's aspirations as a
capital city. As Simon Smithson, who headed
the team from RRP reflected, 'there is a strong
desire here [in Madrid] to raise the profile of
Spain within the European Union.'[5] To this end
an international competition was held in 1997.
It attracted a number of the most successful
architectural practices from around the world,
and was won by a combined team of the
Richard Rogers Partnership and Lamela Studio
of Madrid, and built with engineering by TPS
from the UK and NITEC from Spain.

The resulting building covers 470,200
square metres (5 million square feet) with
thirty-eight gates, while a satellite connected by
underground automatic trains provides a further
287,300 square metres (3 million square feet)
with twenty-six gates. The cost was around
US$1 billion (883.5 million euros). The building
basically consists of three separate structural
systems. The basement sections are solid
concrete, the three storeys above ground
are made of pre-tensioned beams hung
between columns and supporting floor slabs.

TERMINAL BARAJAS T.
ACS FCC Ferrovial

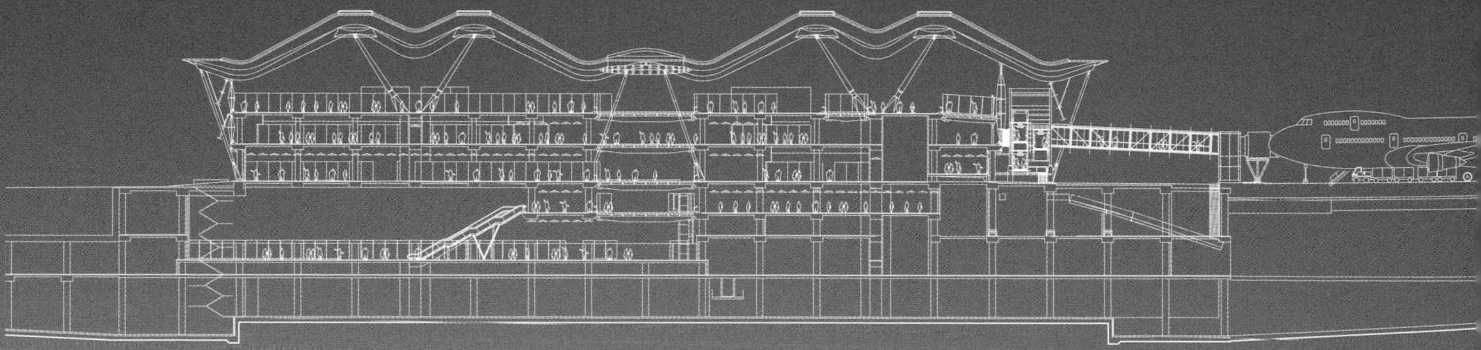

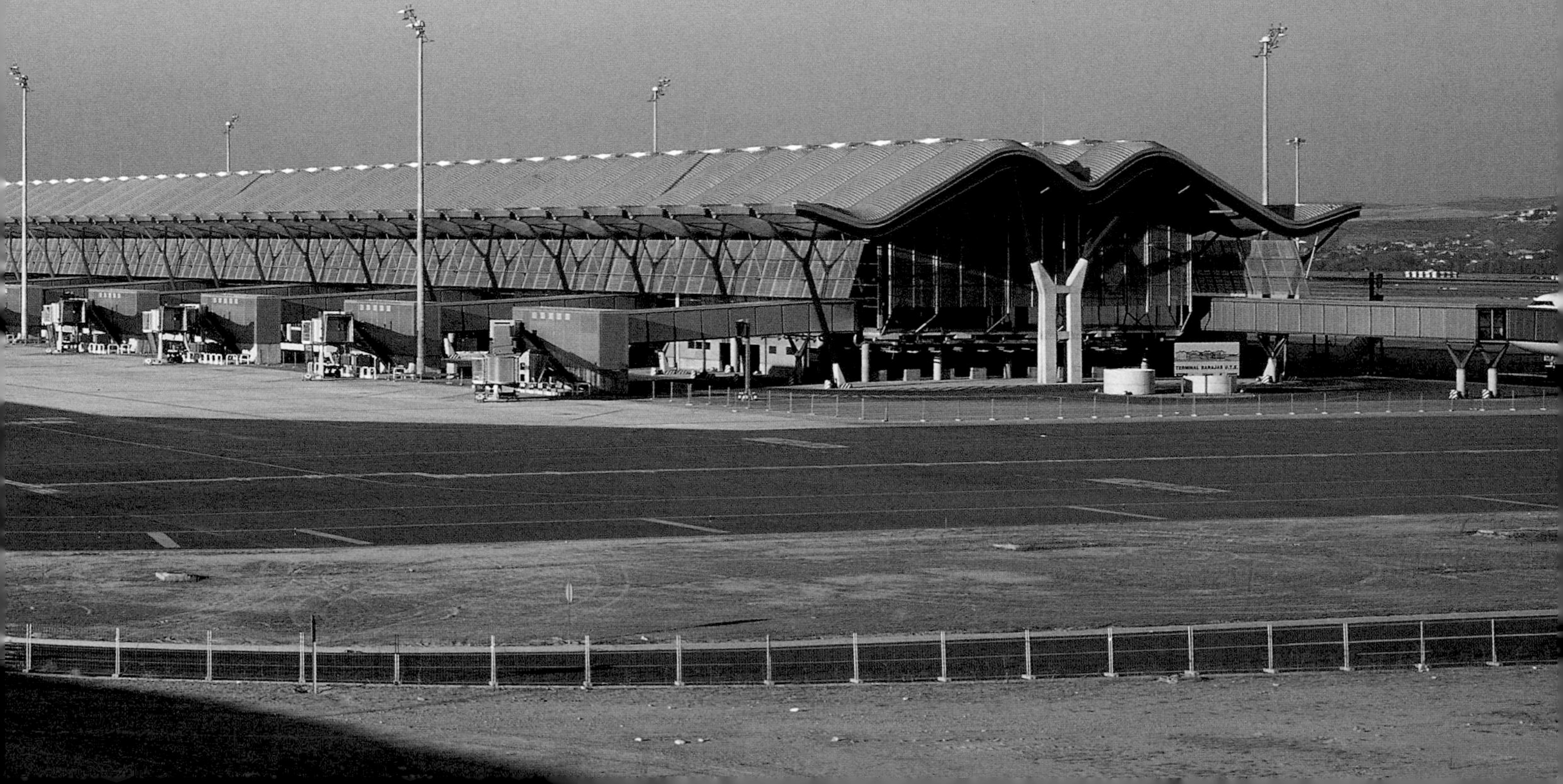
TERMINAL BARAJAS U.T.E.

However, the only section of the structure given any real visual identity is the roof.

The roof structure is designed as an easily extendable module based on an 18 by 9 metre (59 by 29 foot) grid, which was worked out with the assistance of TPS sub-consultants SKM Anthony Hunts of London. Its shape is defined by curved beams set at 9-metre (29-foot) centres forming a gull-wing profile. These consist of three separate steel sections bolted together, in the centre of which is a double S-bend with two arms. The arms taper from 1.5 metres (60 inches) in the middle of each bay to 750 millimetres (30 inches) at each tip – its profile reflects the stress pattern and deeper sections combat areas of greater stress. Each one spans 72 metres (236 feet). They are supported at 18-metre (59-foot) centres by four tapering steel arms bolted to a concrete column laid out in pairs and by Y-shaped canted oval steel hollow sections at their end. Their use reflected the

desire to maximize the large-span, large-volume solution. Carlos Lamela of Studio Lamela explained in a statement that might have been made about Pompidou: 'We were convinced from the beginning that we had to create a large container that would allow as much flexibility as possible.'[6]

Barajas reveals a definite attempt to provide visual clarity through the organization of its spaces. The three concrete storeys of the building are divided into parallel rectangles with linear openings. This allows the separate types of airport processing to be physically split, and as a result the arrivals, check-in, passport control and security checks are on separate islands. In between are glass bridges over canyons lit from above, enabling daylight to penetrate the lower levels of the airport. Above the 'canyons' the spans abut leaving louvred skylights between their tips. These allow visible 'clearings' in the roof 'canopy' to help orientate passengers.

BARAJAS AIRPORT

PREVIOUS SPREAD The design reflects environmental concerns, being part naturally ventilated using a system which delivers air to the occupied levels in the terminal at low velocity. However, while the bamboo cladding of the roof's soffit comes from sustainable sources, its surface is made of energy-expensive aluminium.

BARAJAS AIRPORT

RIGHT Airside – the eaves are supported by Y-shaped columns.

However, walking through the terminal, one is acutely aware that the wider scale of the surrounding space remains difficult to gauge. This is due to the extraordinary horizontality of the design of Barajas. The whole airport sits flat against the landscape. The roofs overhang well beyond the glazed façade and support the glass via a cable-truss system that avoids heavy vertical members. The cable system supports horizontal mullions that hold the weight of the glass and help tie the roof structure to the concrete base below. The canyons provide glimpses into storeys below but give little sense of what each storey contains. Where Kansai and Chek Lap Kok airports each provided a vista that afforded a complete comprehension of the building, at Barajas the views distribute information in stages. The ubiquitous undulating bamboo soffit unifies the building and gives it a more subtle sense of grandeur.

Transport buildings have always been different to any other building type because the length of an individual's occupation is so small and the numbers passing through them so colossal. This has determined that the primary focus of design remains on systems for the processing of people, luggage and freight. Yet unlike industrial buildings, the views and feelings of what is being processed have to be considered. Consequently, transport buildings represent a hybrid form of shed construction. Efficiency and repetition are key but the common units have to be applied in a manner

that is both attractive to the traveller and symbolic for the host country. The stainless steel panels on Kansai are a case in point. They are all the same size in order to clad a huge structure efficiently and relatively cheaply. Yet they are applied to an enormously complex shape in order both to make a room to sit in rather than an endless cavern and to provide a curved shape that symbolizes the aspirations of the Kansai region.

SPORT

SPORT

Spectacle and Symbol

PREVIOUS SPREAD **Sydney International Aquatic Centre**
(Cox Architects)

SYDNEY INTERNATIONAL AQUATIC CENTRE
RIGHT The earth berm indicates where the
temporary seating stood.

Architecture for sport has a distinguished pedigree. The sporting edifices of the Roman Empire were enormously influential buildings. The Colosseum built in Rome in AD 75–80 seated 45,000 people and is the earliest example of the application of the classical language to large buildings. Its influence can by gauged by the fact that it established the standard hierarchy of the orders – Doric, Ionic and Corinthian.

Between the classical period and the 20th century, however, sport inspired rather more modest edifices, with individual sporting clubs and institutions erecting, over time, various utilitarian structures such as clubhouses and banks of spectator-seating to satisfy particular needs. The first generation of Modern Movement architects saw sport as having progressive associations. The sporting aesthetic seemed to fit with the architectural language of the International Style, with its emphasis on austerity, clean shapes and visible structure. In the case of Le Corbusier this involved planning running tracks for the roofs of his buildings, and drawing punch-bags in the perspectives of his flats. But it was only after the Second World War, and the introduction of entirely enclosed sports halls, that sport has once again warranted the construction of complex integrated buildings. Today major sports buildings are civic monuments often built with grand architectural gestures. At the same time more modest sports complexes and swimming pools continue to be housed in cheap and basic structures.

A central distinction in sports buildings lies between those built for watching professionals play, and those in which the general public themselves play. Buildings for spectator sport are far more expensive and reflect the movement of vast numbers of spectators as well as the physical requirements of the sport. Obviously in both cases the shape of the building tends to be determined by the characteristics of the sport. Often this results in simple rectangular boxes, but ever since Kenzo Tange's iconic 1964 Tokyo National Gymnasium, large-span sports architecture has also been used to generate unique and expressionist structures. As a consequence sport inspires both very simple and complex buildings.

The fundamental factor underpinning all sports architecture is the fickle enthusiasm of the public. The best facilities in the world will not attract spectators to a sub-standard contest, and the high maintenance costs of big sports buildings requires that popular contests are staged regularly. The most prestigious and costly international sporting competitions such as the Olympic or Commonwealth Games, or soccer's World and European Cups, have placed the greatest logistical pressures upon their host cities. While several cities, most notably Barcelona, have used the hosting of the Olympic Games as an economic catalyst spurring civic regeneration, the same games have left others saddled with debt. The most notorious example of this was the city of Montreal, whose 1976

hosting of the Olympics was predicted to cost $310 million but actually cost $2 billion, a debt that took thirty years to repay. Hosting any major sports championship invariably involves having to build a number of venues from scratch. Often these are constructed on a scale out of all proportion to any subsequent use. After the 2004 European Cup the Portuguese football club Aveiro was left with a new 30,000-seat stadium. Unfortunately the club only had 5,000 fans.[1] At the same time there are a number of intangible benefits for any city chosen to host such a competition, such as its promotion to 'global destination', attracting new international, as well as national, investment.

At the Olympic Games of 1996 the hosts Atlanta were widely criticized for disregarding the symbolic importance of the games in an undignified quest to maximize short-term revenue from the event. Sydney, by contrast, hosted the subsequent millennium games in 2000 and recognized the need to balance economic success with an attractive presentation of the Olympic ideal. The Sydney Olympics were widely acclaimed. In Britain the *Daily Mirror* declared that: 'for two weeks a nation that truly loves athleticism elevated sport to a plane none of us thought attainable in this cynical world.' In Germany the *Hamburger Adenblatt* declared that: 'The Olympic Movement could not have found a better place for its rebirth.'[2] And in the USA *Time* magazine commented that:

'Australians can now allow themselves the quiet satisfaction of knowing that they have thrown the best party in the world.'[3]

For reasons both of economy and security many of Sydney's new facilities were built on a large detached site to the west of the city at Homebush Park. It is now becoming apparent, however, that quite apart from their hefty cost some of the these facilities will be underused in future years despite Australia's sporting culture. Those that have succeeded have certain characteristics in common with more utilitarian community buildings. They can serve their respective sport at a wide variety of levels, with facilities for both national and local teams. Or they have the capacity to house completely different activities altogether.

One of the first buildings built at Homebush Park was **Sydney International**

Aquatic Centre designed by Cox Architects in association with Peddle Thorp, and its construction made a key contribution to the success of Sydney's bid. Built as a 5,000-seat swimming centre it has served both national and community requirements. The Aquatic Centre's plan was conceived by placing a rectangle within the confines of a circle and truncating either end along the lines of the resulting curves. The roof has a vault, curved in cross-section, that runs the entire length of the building. This is supported all along one wall by a 135-metre (443-foot) longitudinal arch. This arch enabled the wall to be removed during the Olympics to accommodate 10,000 additional seats allowing a much larger capacity crowd to watch the swimming events than would ever be assembled again. After the Olympics the Aquatic Centre successfully shrunk

back to its original size and is not now over-scaled for its current function.

The building is entered via a massive earth berm, which originally supported the temporary Olympic seating. A 51.5- by 25-metre (169- by 82-foot) competition pool forms the focus of the main space, but there is also a 33-metre by 25-metre utility pool primarily used for diving, a 50- by 18.2-metre (82- by 60-foot) training pool with a moveable floor for lap swimming and water polo, and a 900 square metre (9,700 square foot) free-form leisure pool. The centre also accommodates competitor, visitor and club changing rooms, electronic timing, officials' rooms, a gymnasium and a restaurant.

At Homebush Park the Olympic gymnastics and basketball events were held in the **Sydney Superdome**. Also designed by Cox Architects this building follows the trends of an

increasing number of sports buildings: it has a roof. Sport at this scale is heavily funded by the sale of television rights, which places extra demands upon scheduling events irrespective of the weather. The Superdome consists of three components. First, it houses Australia's largest covered arena, with 15,000 seats surrounding an event floor of over 3,600 square metres (38,800 square feet). A further 5,000 seats can be added by opening a temporary lower tier. An office and foyer structure wraps around one side of this arena, and on the other it is abutted by a 3,500-spot car park.

The stadium is supported by 24 steel masts 42 metres (138 feet) tall, which radiate around the top of the structure. These support a tension ring from which a lightweight steel roof is hung. This spans 140 by 100 metres (459 by 328 feet), with a roof area of 12,500 square metres (135,000 square feet). The foyer is covered by a separate roof that curves asymmetrically around two sides of the stadium. Structurally it is strutted off the main stadium by triangular trusses formed from the combination of two prefabricated planar trusses. A veranda extends the foyer towards Olympic Boulevard and protects its full-height glazing from the sun. The veranda rests on delicate tree-like split columns of tubular steel 14 metres (46 feet) high and placed at 13-metre (43-foot) centres. These thin columns split into four even thinner diagonal supports that prop thin ridge beams. These, in conjunction with the masts and tension cables on the roof above, reduce the

sense of this enormous building's scale along its public entrance.

The Superdome cost 197 million Australian dollars, 60 million of which was contributed by the private sector in return for the right to run the venue for thirty years. If the money is recouped it will be because this is the most multi-functional Olympic facility at Homebush. Because it is essentially a huge covered space it has already accommodated functions as diverse as supercross, tennis, rock concerts, religious services, school spectaculars and banquets. Of all Sydney's underused Olympic sporting facilities the large-span envelope solution has already proved itself the most adaptable to change. However, the operational costs of such a venue remain enormous. Despite being one of busiest venues of this kind in the world it fell into receivership in July 2004, and was bought by the Acer Computing company in March 2006, and swiftly renamed the Acer Arena.

The symmetrical nature of sports pitches and the stringent safety regulations in the control of crowds have encouraged diagrammatic design solutions that simplify the shapes of sports buildings. However, sports facilities also have a visual presence that is often central to the sports presentation. In the case of the new Wembley Stadium designed by Foster and Partners and HOK Lobb Architects, it was obvious that the iconic towers of the original would have to be replaced, in this case with an oversailing arch. The image of the building was

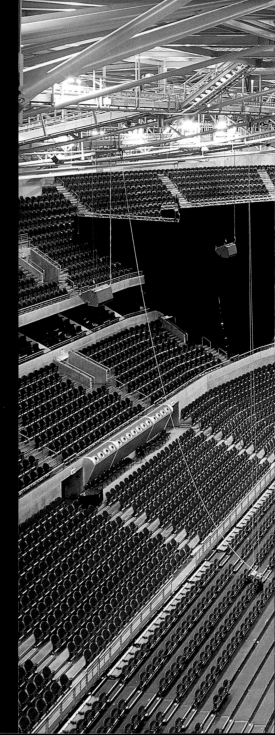

NATIONAL CENTRE FOR
RHYTHMIC GYMNASTICS
RIGHT Concrete and steel are used
interchangeably in this structure.

recognized as a integral component in the profile
of the sport.

The **National Centre for Rhythmic
Gymnastics**, Alicante, Spain, designed by Enric
Miralles and his then partner Carme Pinós, was
designed to provide gymnastics with a striking
visual symbol. It was built to provide practice and
competition facilities for Spain's gymnasts and to
host the International Championships in 1993.
Miralles and Pinós could turn this brief into a
building of great geometric complexity and
individualism because gymnastics does not
require a symmetrical pitch but an open space
that is then laid out with a variety of mats and
equipment depending upon the event.
Consequently the architects determined to
create a new building type for gymnasts, one that
would deter later appropriation by other sports
such as five-a-side football or basketball.

Miralles and Pinós used the topography
of the site to inspire the form of their designs.
They sought a correspondence between the
shape of the building and patterns visible in the
surrounding landscape. The Centre is sited on the
northeast slope of a hill behind the town of
Alicante and faces out over a valley inland from
the coast surrounded by a number of sports
pitches. The structure of the building is very
difficult to comprehend from the outside, or even
in places from the inside, consisting of seemingly
independent elements. It houses training rooms,
gyms, open halls, a cafeteria and two large venues,
one for training, the other for competition.

In general terms the plan is ordered by two triangular forms overlaid in a rough 'T' shape, both of which are cut into the descending slope of the hill. Each triangle houses a major sports space. The first, lying roughly east–west, is the gymnastics training area. This space is penetrated by two structures. The first is made up of a set of cantilevered concrete planes that support glass bricks concealing the changing rooms. The second is a rectangular steel-clad corridor held on a slight diagonal by a single concrete column capped by a triangular steel prop. This contains a public access ramp that leads directly from the ground outside up to the first floor. It is equipped with windows allowing spectators queueing for the event glimpses of the gymnasts training below.

The second triangular shape, running north–south, contains the competition stadium.

This is only roughly rectangular in plan as the eastern wall is skewed as if to accommodate the hillside behind. Banks of seating for 4,000 spectators set on concrete stepped plinths surround the room. These banks of seats are free of the rigid geometry usually determined by rectangular sports pitches and are not arranged in a uniform way. Instead they reflect the uneven distribution of different groups of spectators, whose places are determined in advance. The lower part of the eastern stand is for Sports Federation members. The short block to the north is for relatives of competitors, the one to the south for the press. The only symmetrical stand, the largest, is allocated for the general public. This stand can be seen on the façade of the back of the building propped up by a row of concrete columns. This back view, facing west, provides the one symmetrical element in the

NATIONAL CENTRE FOR
RHYTHMIC GYMNASTICS
PREVIOUS SPREAD A series of trusses runs along the roof line – the height of the trusses gives an idea of the breadth of the span.

NATIONAL CENTRE FOR
RHYTHMIC GYMNASTICS
OPPOSITE Changing rooms on concrete planes penetrate the training area.

NATIONAL CENTRE FOR
RHYTHMIC GYMNASTICS
ABOVE The entrance rampway passes through the training area; the windows provide glimpses of the gymnasts warming up to compete.

RIGHT **Banked seating in the competition
stadium. The north stand, in the
foreground, is for competitors' friends
and relatives; beyond it is the main
stand, for the general public.**

whole scheme and serves as its public face, seen
as visitors climb up the hill from the town.

In between these two sports spaces a zone
of circulation space forms a route across the
scheme. Various additional functions are also
located here, including offices, toilets and
changing rooms. On the first floor, ramps to the
west and staircases to the east funnel spectators
into the building and provide views over the
main spaces, while the ground floor is solely the
preserve of the gymnasts.

The architects have chosen to mix
structural systems at will. Concrete and steel are
used interchangeably. Huge chunks of concrete
support the stairs, steel ramps lie directly on top
of a hefty concrete base. The outside of the
building is a dizzy array of structure at times so
oversized as to function practically as sculpture.
Different elements appear to have an
independent relationship with the landscape,
almost accidentally interlocking to form the
building. Very few secondary surfaces are
applied, pre-cast elements remain quite
autonomous, in-situ concrete is left very rough.

The one ordering device of the entire
scheme is a low-pitched roof. This is supported by
three steel trusses that run along the longitudinal
axis and are visible from around the site. They are
a deliberately low-tech feature with their wide
flat flanges of steel resembling a funfair ride more
than the work of a technologist like Grimshaw or
Foster. The individual steel box girders that make
up the profile are constructed so that their

dimensions reflect the load being carried – and thus, the largest span, over the sports hall, can be seen from afar. Their profile also echoes the distant profile of the mountains beyond.

Inside, the soffit is covered by a secondary structure of down-standing bow-shaped trusses. While these ensure a flat roof surface, they also clutter it, an effect partially relieved by the addition of colourful canvas sheets. These hang on the undersides of the trusses and add a festival note of gaiety. The roofs are supported

in the centre of the training area by a tripod of steel columns, and on the periphery by concrete columns.

From an architect's perspective the building's crude detailing is part of its attraction, the whole feeling like a huge architectural model. Miralles and Pinós understood the tactile pleasure inherent in the materials, and chose to emphasize the building's rough-and-ready approximations. The broad sweep of the roof, for example, did not completely cover the north and

south corners of the sports hall. To the north additional triangular trusses carry the roof over the spectators. The southern corner has an entirely different roof structure.

The building's design shows an alternative approach to that of an engineered-aesthetic of perfect efficiency. Different elements of the building are engineered independently; there is no hint of the concerns with economy and precision that were dominating sports structures built around the same time. The intention is

rather something individual and sculptural,
based on the artistic personalities of the
architects. This proved problematic when, just
before this building started on site, Miralles and
Pinós went their separate ways taking both jobs
and elements of their joint graphic style with
them. But what this project proved is that the
large-volume aspects of sports architecture
could be manipulated into more idiosyncratic
forms than the pursuit of the simplest and most
comprehensible diagram.

Miralles would go on to find, in the controversy which surrounded his Scottish Parliament building, that it is far harder to sell the idea of a project based on individual genius than it is to sell a type of architecture which stresses the efficiency of its engineering and technology.

Important sports buildings are designed to house major events, but much of our experience of actually playing sport also involves large-volume structures. Simple sports boxes and leisure centres are found on the outskirts of cities and towns in the developed world. The vast majority are very simple and are often almost entirely artificially lit. One of the rare exceptions where this basic form is given a sophisticated architectural expression is that of the **Buchholz Sports Centre** completed in 1998 in Uster, Switzerland, by the architects Camenzind Gräfensteiner. Just like the Crystal Palace and Galerie des Machines, the essential idea of this building is that of a steel structure visible through surrounding glass walls. Like these early structures the result is an extruded shape supported by a series of identical arches.

The Buchholz Sports Centre accommodates a three-pitch sports hall along with seating for a thousand spectators. Camenzind Gräfensteiner chose to implement a very simple diagram. A concrete plinth contains the pitches and provides a raised and banked level of spectator-seating above changing rooms and services. Various detached volumes sit

above this plinth and contain ancillary functions such as a lift tower, a press-room and a warm-up hall. The steel structural members rest on the concrete plinth and the whole structure is then clad in glass, completed with a monopitched, grass-covered roof.

The building has great visual clarity. The welded steel frames have three pin-joints and are anchored onto the concrete plinth. The pin-

BUCHHOLZ SPORTS CENTRE
OPPOSITE This side elevation shows translucent glass above the concrete plinth.

BUCHHOLZ SPORTS CENTRE
ABOVE A ramp leads up to the entrance.

BUCHHOLZ SPORTS CENTRE
FOLLOWING SPREAD The same essential idea of a steel structure visible through glass dates back to the Crystal Palace (1851) and Galerie des Machines (1889).

BUCHHOLZ SPORTS CENTRE

ABOVE The sports centre encloses a 65 by 27 metre (213 by 89 foot) multi-purpose sports pitch.

BUCHHOLZ SPORTS CENTRE

OPPOSITE Portal frames are anchored onto the concrete plinth.

joints are positioned so that the movement forces are greatest in the junction at the top of the north façade. Here the girder is both widest and highest, leaning out over the front of the building at the highest point of the monopitched roof. The steel trusses enclose the minimum height and width requirements in the brief, resulting in considerable efficiency in terms of building costs and future maintenance. The glass cladding is translucent to the east and west and transparent to the north and south. During the day the building receives a great amount of natural light — even on cloudy days and at night its simple structure, seen through the glass, advertises the activities within. The translucency of the east and west façades allow the sun shading to be integrated into the glazing unit. The building is naturally ventilated through horizontal air-vents lying below the east, west and north

façades. In summer the vents are also opened during the night to cool the concrete plinth so that it serves as a thermal store during the day.

The Sports Centre at Uster follows conventional diagrammatic thinking in using the symmetry of the sports pitches to establish a geometry that determines the building's structure. When it won the prestigious Europe-wide Bauwelt Prize in 1999 the judges praised its simplicity: 'as well as making the most of limited means, [it is] designed for function rather than for design's sake.'[4] In many ways these comments could stand for any building of this type. This building succeeds, more specifically, by making its simple character extremely explicit. Its lucid construction expresses the sporting aspirations of the people of Uster quite as successfully as Miralles and Pinós's conveys the aspirations of the Spanish gymnastics team.

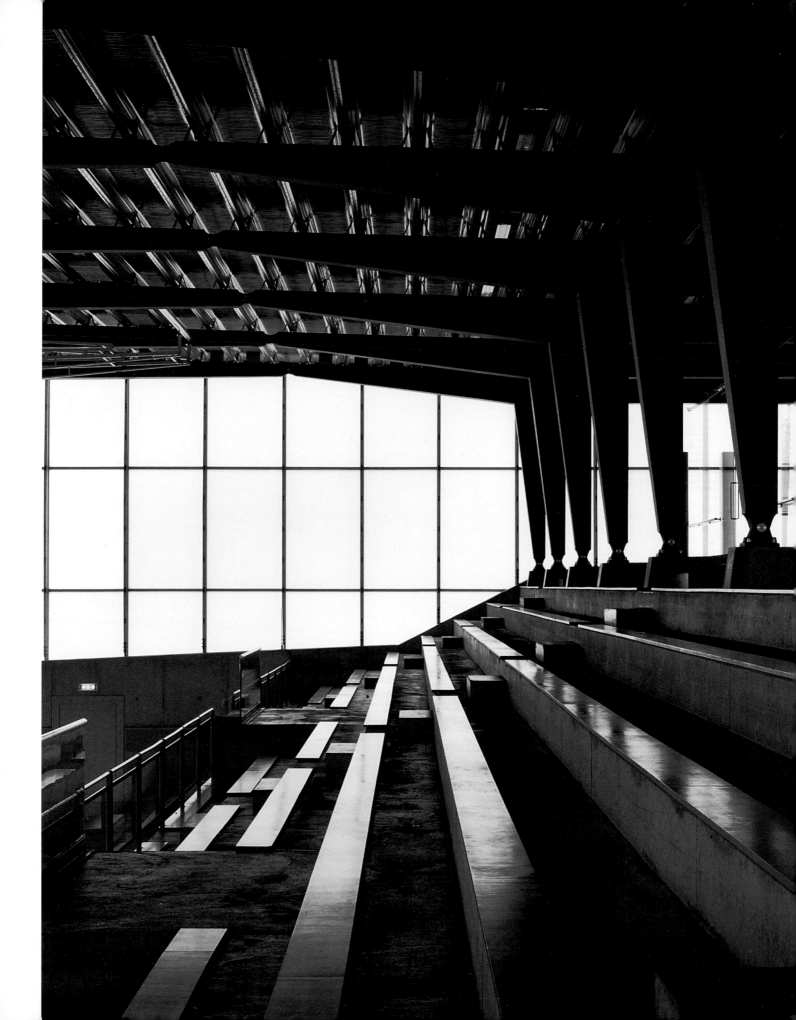

ARTS

ARTS
Customizing the Shed

During the 20th century, in the absence of major ecclesiastical buildings, architects generally considered arts projects their most prestigious commissions. Such clients have often proved amenable to a large degree of innovation and have encouraged visually arresting design. This has provided great opportunities for experimentation and has resulted in many influential new buildings.

Perhaps the most influential of all 20th-century arts buildings was Jørn Utzon's Sydney Opera House. Built between 1959 and 1973, it challenged the dominance of rectilinear forms in the Modern Movement. The building's fourteen-year construction saw the budget climb tenfold and Utzon left Sydney before the project was complete. Nevertheless, the Opera House has become such a powerful symbol of the city that these problems now seem irrelevant. It was the first unusual-shaped-building as city-dominating icon. It did for Sydney what the Statue of Liberty did for New York. In seconds anyone looking at a photograph could tell where it was. Today, it is rivalled only by Uluru (Ayres Rock) as the primary symbol of Australia.

The Opera House demonstrated that arts projects could achieve iconic status, and since then many other factors have also led architects to create dramatic visual symbols. The general unpopularity of much of the orthodox modernism of the 1960s and 1970s encouraged architects to differentiate themselves from their immediate predecessors. Most of the opprobrium was directed at the anonymous and insensitive concrete blocks that became the staple diet of the post-war building boom. Consequently, the less rectangular a new building, the better. Since the beginning of the 1990s a rapid improvement in computer modelling software has made it easier to construct complex shapes. This has given architects greater practical freedom to tackle relatively unusual forms on an acceptable budget.

Today the media also fashions certain architects into celebrities. To some extent this has always happened. Pevsner had complained in *Pioneers of Modern Design* about 'the craving of the public for the surprising and fantastic.'[1] But the quantity and range of media that mention architects has increased dramatically since then. Architects with very clear signature styles have the advantage of making work that is easier to recognize. By doing so these architects create effective brands, and the more individual the visual identity, the stronger will be the recognition of that brand. Recent international architectural competitions have reinforced this effect. While competitions have become more common, they now tend to be 'limited', with a specific 'guest list' of invited architects rather than being open to anyone. All these factors have encouraged architects to design museums and auditoriums in exciting expressionist forms. Since the enormous popularity of the Pompidou Centre, the buildings themselves have often become a bigger attraction than their contents. Meanwhile, the range of requirements for cultural buildings has expanded. Museums now have to cope with the escalating demands of modern art: pieces that come in an enormous variety of scales or else are made in a huge range of media. Music venues now have to accommodate a proliferation of different musical genres: tonal and atonal, electric and acoustic. At the same time commercial pressures have added retail functions to venues. Both museums and music centres are now also expected to include extensive café and retail space as well as greater facilities for education.

The most successful recent arts building, in terms both of its international financial draw and of the effect it had on its designer's career, is the **Guggenheim Museum** at Bilbao This is the product of an explicit deal uniting a global brand with a prosperous but fundamentally unglamorous city. Bilbao also had political aspirations towards providing the Basque region with greater independence from Madrid. Thus, there was a strategic and symbolic subtext to establishing direct links with foreign institutions.

In April 1991 the Guggenheim Museum in New York approached a member of Bilbao's treasury department. Under the controversial directorship of Thomas Krens, the Guggenheim had already approached a number of European cities asking whether they would be interested in buying a franchise of the museum. Their idea was that while host cities would build their own

PREVIOUS SPREAD **GUGGENHEIM MUSEUM**
Seen from the river the Guggenheim's lone column refers to an architectural language otherwise ignored.

GUGGENHEIM MUSEUM
ABOVE The curved shapes of the atrium from which galleries are accessed.

GUGGENHEIM MUSEUM
OPPOSITE The west wing, the building's largest, is 130 metres (427 feet) long.

museums and pay for the franchises, the artistic direction would come from New York. The Guggenheim would decide what the Bilbao museum would buy, what it would exhibit and how it would advertise.[2] The deal proposed that two regional governments would pay for the construction and maintenance of the museum and the Guggenheim would loan it work while its own collection was purchased. The president of the Basque government went

to New York to hand over the $20 million cheque himself.

The construction of the building became part of a huge development programme in Bilbao involving a new airport terminal and footbridge by Santiago Calatrava, new metro stations by Norman Foster, a new conference and performing arts centre by Federico Soriano and a new business district developed by César Pelli. The Guggenheim would serve as the honey-pot in the centre of the scheme. It was intended to attract tourists and generate fresh interest in Spain's fourth largest city.

Krens chose a friend of his, the American architect Frank Gehry, to design the Guggenheim. Gehry understood the need to make an iconic building. He overlaid a relatively orthodox stone-clad building with a series of wave-like sculptural titanium shapes.

The public descend into the museum from the south via a long staircase. They arrive in a central atrium that overlooks the river and is surrounded by galleries. Behind them the orthogonal south wing houses the permanent collection in two levels of conventional galleries, each consisting of three linked rooms. To the west lies what Gehry calls 'the boat', the longest titanium-clad gallery running parallel to the river and under the road bridge. It is 130 metres (427 feet) long, with a ceiling that rises from 12 metres (40 feet) to 26 metres (85 feet). Opposite it is the smaller east wing, also housed in an organic metal shape. This contains smaller

GUGGENHEIM MUSEUM
OPPOSITE The Guggenheim's titanium skin
instantly ensured its iconic status.

galleries and public facilities overlooking the harbour. There are also additional petal-shaped galleries, which jut out around the atrium, again clad in titanium.

The popularity of the project owes much to the combined effect of these sculptural shapes and their titanium cladding. The conventional orthogonal parts of the building, by comparison, command less attention and are consequently photographed much less often. It is the highly reflective titanium skin that gives these loose organic shapes a coherent visual image, one that contrasts very effectively with the dour industrial city around it. While the art inside is typical of corporate America, the juxtaposition of the building with its environment is the most striking since Pompidou, and achieved without the advantages of Paris as its backdrop.

The Guggenheim in Bilbao has been an enormously successful financial investment. It cost $100 million, cheap when compared to the $700 million the city spent on the first line of their metro. It attracted an extra 1.3 million visitors to the city in the first year followed by 1.1 million and 3 million in the subsequent two years. Within two years tourist revenues had increased by $400 million. Even during the year after 11 September 2001 the museum still attracted over 800,000 visitors to the city. However, it was the motivation behind the project that caused controversy. Krens himself defined the necessary criteria for an iconic museum in fairly mercenary terms. For him an

art museum was 'a theme park with four attractions: good architecture, a good permanent collection, primary and secondary art exhibitions, and amenities such as shops and restaurants.'[3] Indeed, Krens made little effort to disguise the economics at work. In both New York and Bilbao he put on a show of the dresses of Giorgio Armani in exchange for $12 million, a deal described by *The New York Times* as, 'a short sighted exchange of cash for dignity'.

Krens's rapid expansion of the Guggenheim empire has not been equally successful outside Bilbao. While he succeeded in building in Las Vegas and Berlin, plans for an ambitious part-underwater Guggenheim in Rio de Janeiro designed by Jean Nouvel were eventually scrapped. Similarly a downtown New York design again by Gehry was put on hold after a SoHo, NYC version folded. According to critic Deyan Sudjic, the Guggenheim in Bilbao 'stripped away a lot of the alibis for building museums, revealing the egotism and showmanship beneath the rhetoric of self-improvement and scholarship.'[4] But if Krens has not come out of the expansion programme with his reputation entirely intact, his favourite architect, Frank Gehry, certainly has. Gehry went on to complete the **Walt Disney Concert Hall** in Los Angeles, another project clad in a wavy shiny metal skin.

Reflective metal cladding, however, proved problematic in downtown LA. The stainless steel used here looks as spectacular as the

Guggenheim's titanium, but there are consequences in placing a shiny object in ever-sunny California that were avoided in the rain-swept north coast of Spain. Apartments surrounding the concert hall experienced an alarming rise in temperature. As a result sections of the stainless steel had to be de-shined in order to reduce the glare.

While Disney was finally completed six years after the Bilbao Guggenheim in 2003, it had in fact been designed before it. Gehry won the limited competition in 1988 but it took eleven years before work on site commenced. The concert hall, which has 2,265 seats, was completed for an official cost of $274 million. Minoru Nagata and Yasuhisa Toyota of Nagata Acoustics engineered its acoustics. It takes an expressive shape, supposedly the 'direct expression of acoustical parameters'[5] – as if a literal model of Ernest Fennella's 'frozen music'. But this is a little far-fetched. The acoustic engineer started with a simple rectangular box-like shape and Gehry kept the box but added concave and convex internal walls for visual effect.

Both buildings were immediately acclaimed as masterpieces by the American press. *The New York Times*'s architectural critic Herbert Muschamp described the Guggenheim at Bilbao as standing, 'for an American style of freedom. That style is voluptuous, emotional, intuitive and exhibitionist. It is mobile, fluid, material, mercurial, fearless, radiant and as

WALT DISNEY CONCERT HALL

WALT DISNEY CONCERT HALL

ABOVE Swirling forms are famously designed
using the CATIA CAD programme used in
the aeroplane industry. However, the
skin is in fact a series of stainless steel
overlapping shingles manually adjusted
by workmen on site.

WALT DISNEY CONCERT HALL

OPPOSITE The stainless steel cladding is striking
but practically problematic, since it can
create a lot of glare.

fragile as a newborn child.'[6] For Muschamp it
was not simply an icon but an American icon.
He declared that: 'If you want to look into the
heart of American art today, you are going to
need a passport.' Certainly, as Muschamp
astutely recognized, there was nothing
meaningfully Basque or Spanish about the
Guggenheim in Bilbao. It was also, in the best
American tradition, hugely populist: 'It is almost
Shakespearean in its ability to appeal across the
social spectrum.'[7] But for Muschamp the origins
of the achievement specifically lay in American
know-how. In fact Muschamp declared that: 'The
use of the computer on this project challenges
the whole construct of order and method
coming out of the Renaissance'.[8] For Muschamp
the new epoch ushered in by the Guggenheim
was one founded upon its technological
credentials, specifically the use of the computer

in the design process. It is presented as a self-
conscious work of art but one by a master of
technology.

Gehry Partners' use of computer modelling
technology to build these elaborate shapes has
been highly publicized. It is well known that they
were designed using a French computer program
CATIA, which had been used to design the
Mirage fighter plane and Boeing 777. This has
encouraged visitors to assume that these
buildings have a similar level of technological
sophistication to the latest aircraft. William J.
Mitchell, writing about how Gehry designs and
builds, described his technique as: 'an exploration
of a formal universe that was no less rigorously
logical and mathematically elegant than that of
ancient Greek geometry, but which – as a
practical matter – had been inaccessible before
computer-graphics technology unlocked it.'[9]

WALT DISNEY CONCERT HALL
PREVIOUS SPREAD Gehry's free-flowing volumes contrast
with the orthogonal frames of LA
tower blocks.

WALT DISNEY CONCERT HALL
OPPOSITE The shapes reflect personal choice
rather than ideal geometrics.

However, this issue deserves closer scrutiny. These forms were not determined as an engineered response to the brief. They were devised by the means of physical models that were first scanned and then converted into CAD. Gehry's shapes are therefore a reflection of personal choice in objects fashioned purely sculpturally by hand rather than ideal geometries derived from mathematics. But what is significant are the lengths to which Gehry's shapes have to be justified in terms of elegant mathematics and rigorous logic, rather than just as powerful artistic forms. Ultimately, for his apologists it is important to explain Gehry's buildings as products of scientific innovation as well as artistic vision. A closer look at the structure of, say, Disney reveals that it is not as technologically radical as it might at first seem. The wild swirling stainless steel skin is in fact supported by a skeleton structure simply constructed from a mixture of standard I-beams, square and circular tubes. It is divided into a grid, every single square of which is cross-braced. All of these members are bolted together. The result is a very dense heavy frame. The shapes supported by the frame may look complex but the means by which they are achieved are fairly rudimentary.

The second assumption about CATIA and its use in the aeroplane manufacture is that, like aeroplanes, Gehry's work would be manufactured to finer tolerances than mere products of the building industry. Actually CATIA could not be used to cut and form the metal sheet in the manner of computer cutting.[10] Instead it simply determined the location of panels. The skin is, in fact, made up of giant overlapping shingles, which allow for plenty of adjustment by workmen on site. When a new opaque surface had to be added to the Walt Disney Concert Hall to reduce the problem of glare, it was simply attached between the panels. However, CATIA was used to shape the double curvature surfaces in the limestone of the seemingly more conventional orthogonal parts of the building. Where computer-aided design was used in an innovative way was in ensuring the manufacturing process was extremely efficient.

The third assumption is that these metal skins are in themselves technologically cutting-edge. In Bilbao the use of titanium was explained as a consequence of its strength and durability, but perhaps the primary motive was its exoticism. It was chosen only after a fortuitous international crash in the price of the metal. The sheets of titanium are fixed to a lightweight secondary frame of open sections of galvanized steel. It is galvanized steel that determines the position and thus the shape of the flowing curves.

Thus, while these buildings are idiosyncratic, they also have shed-like characteristics. Steel frames clad with metal sheathing determine their shape. The same fascination with technological cladding evident in buildings by Foster and Grimshaw is also evident here. If the tube shape of the Sainsbury Centre established that the roofs and walls could be clad identically, Gehry's curves blur the boundary between roof and wall completely. While the internal spaces are not neutral, but are functionally designed, they take the form of a dominant single storey under a lightweight roof. Gehry's architecture has not so much replaced the big shed as customized it to produce sculptural forms and, like the work of the 'High-Tech' pioneers, it is an architecture whose technological credentials form part of its presentation.

Perhaps the only member of the current international array of super-successful architects whose buildings are as easily identifiable as Frank Gehry's is Daniel Libeskind. Libeskind's career took off in 1989 when, after a successful but wholly academic career, he unexpectedly won an international competition for an extension to the Jewish Museum in Berlin. After considerable political wrangling the museum eventually opened in 2001. Libeskind's design strategy mixed an incomprehensible formal technique with an emotional presentation that fully embraced the tragic subject matter. Its characteristic diagonal slit windows, according to Libeskind, are the consequence of drawing lines on a map of Berlin between the houses of prominent Jews. These lines were then elevated onto the façades of the building.

WALT DISNEY CONCERT HALL
OPPOSITE The stainless steel skin is supported by
a skeleton structure constructed from
standard steel members.

As *Architectural Record* described in its review, 'Berlin's contradictory history – aspiration and accomplishment versus repression and tragedy – is almost literally written all over the building's façades.' But the appearance of the façades of the Jewish Museum also suggested that some advanced scientific research had been involved in its design. *Architectural Record* mused that: 'The gestures of form and pattern appear to be the product of a mathematical formula. Libeskind, though, does not expose his compositional process to scrutiny. Although the code seems knowable, the design is disturbing because its sources remain unrevealed.'[11] Thus what is 'disturbing' about the design of this building is that while there appears to be a logic to its fenestration, that logic is incomprehensible. What is certain is that it is impossible to fathom the design of the slits when using them as windows. Instead the visitor is expected to relate the zig-zag plan and diagonal window patterns to the victims of the Holocaust because that is the explanation provided. How this actually happens is unclear, but we are expected to assume that it's profound. Libeskind's pronouncements certainly made him sound clever: 'I thought of this [the Jewish Museum] as a living presence. History is not over.'[12] And as Libeskind's autobiography made clear, the author of the Jewish Museum was no ordinary man but had grown up a child prodigy who did his homework while he walked home.[13]

Certainly with such an emotive subject matter any effective critique of the building was always going to be fraught with difficulties. The Jewish Museum became very famous, as did Daniel Libeskind, and he went on to design the **Imperial War Museum North (IWM-N)** in Manchester.

Libeskind's basic idea for the IWM-N can be seen in a diagram on show inside the building. It is based on a metaphor of 'the contemporary world shattered into fragments and reassembled as a fundamental emblem of conflict.'[14] This results in three convex chunks, or 'shards', taken from the shape of the globe. These are described as representing the air, water and earth – each of which has served as a theatre of war. The air shard forms the tower, the earth shard the exhibition space and the water shard the café. Libeskind has also claimed that the form of the building was partially generated by views of the site from points in the city: from the Old Trafford Football Stadium, the Lowry Centre and the Manchester Ship Canal. But the relationship between these two ordering systems remains unclear.

The result is a series of spiky shapes reminiscent of other buildings by Libeskind, including the Jewish Museum in Berlin. These 'shards' were more fully articulated in the competition scheme. After this, various expected sources of funding did not materialize and the scheme had to be downsized from £42 million ($62 million) to £30 million ($46

million). Rather than start again from first principles the size of the shards was reduced, and their form re-shaped. Each 'shard' is constructed from steel frames with substantial spans enclosing large spaces clad in standard Kalzip system panels.

As a result, only the building's peculiar shape distinguishes it from the stores and warehouses that predominate in this part of the city.

On closer inspection there are consistent details, such as the seams of the roof cladding that follow the 'longitude' of the shape. But the building remains a very simple shed. The air-shard tower acts as signboard for the scheme and contains nothing except a lift that takes visitors to a high level viewing-platform to look out over Manchester.

The permanent exhibition space located in the largest space, the 'earth shard', places exhibits in a room of clashing acute angles and long slit lights set at diagonals. The floor gently curves underfoot to intensify the disconcerting sensation. The shed envelope is skilfully combined with the design of the exhibition. The result is a shed built with the rhetoric of an exhibition stand.

On the outside its slick metal cladding assists the overall visual effect of clashing 'shards'. But rather than conjuring up the idea of pieces of the globe in conflict, they are more strongly reminiscent of pieces of the other similarly clad metal sheds which litter this urban hinterland. This is 'Ikea store in conflict'.

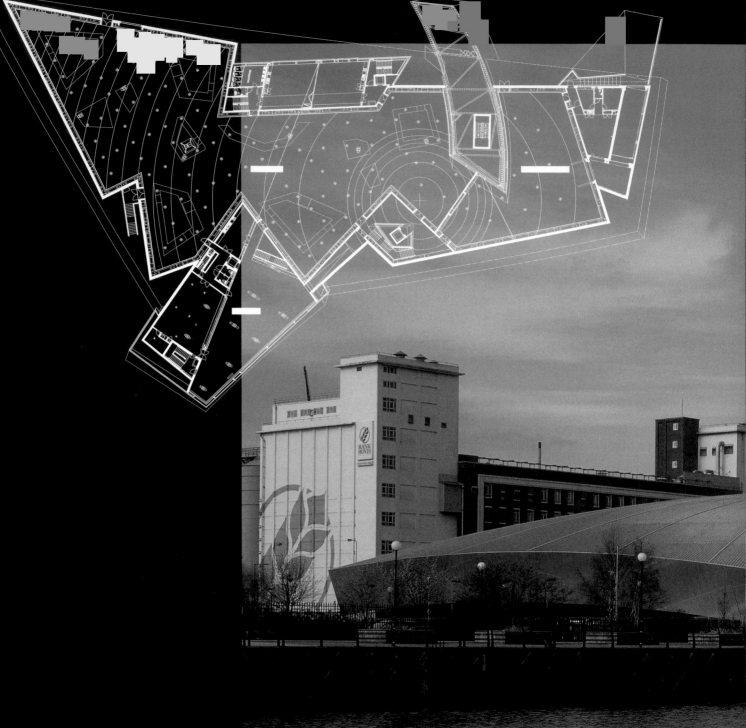

IMPERIAL WAR MUSEUM NORTH (IWM-N)
RIGHT Supposedly derived from pieces of a
shattered globe, the museum building is
also reminiscent of cheap out-of-town
architecture, a consequence of its very
limited budget.

welcome
to the
watershard café

watch the world go by whilst
experiencing relaxing views over
the Manchester Ship Canal • enjoy a
fresh cream cake with a cup of tea or
indulge in a freshly prepared meal

IMPERIAL WAR MUSEUM NORTH (IWM-N)
LEFT The café. Every opportunity has been taken
to pursue Libeskind's signature vocabulary
of spiky forms.

Any scepticism one might have felt about
the meaning inherent in the slit windows of the
Jewish Museum, or the literal gesture of bits of
the planet piercing each other, was compounded
when Libeskind designed a Graduate Centre for
the University of North London in the same
language of intersecting spiky objects. As Ellis
Woodman of *Building Design* concluded with
evident frustration after an interview with
Libeskind spent trying to get him to explain the
similarities of style but differences of function:
'The formal expression of the Graduate Centre
struck me as completely of a piece with that
of the "crisis buildings" [Jewish Museum and
IWM-N]. Surely, it is not possible to take his
claims for the significance of those earlier
projects seriously, now that the same tricks have
been rolled out to serve this 'secular' brief.'[15]

What is most striking about Libeskind's
buildings are their stylistic similarities, their
common grammar of gestures. In many ways
they do for the shed what Philip Johnson did for
the skyscraper when he built the AT&T Building
in the shape of a Chippendale highboy in 1984.
At IWM-N, Libeskind takes the industrial shed
and dresses it up as expressionist sculpture, just
as Johnson dressed the skyscraper in the cloak
of post-modernism.

Curiously, in one or two cases Libeskind's
technique appears to have been employed by
other architects as well. A similar language of
sharp fragments can be seen in the architecture
of **Federation Square** in Melbourne.

Big Picture

am, 2pm, 5pm

2 noon, 3pm

1pm, 4pm

friend
fiend

alisation   peace

A war does not end with the

goods entrance

IMPERIAL WAR MUSEUM NORTH (IWM-N)

PREVIOUS SPREAD LEFT — The 'air-shard' tower takes visitors up to a view over the canal.

IMPERIAL WAR MUSEUM NORTH (IWM-N)

PREVIOUS SPREAD RIGHT — The exhibition design is closely integrated with the architecture.

IMPERIAL WAR MUSEUM NORTH (IWM-N)

LEFT — The 'water-shard' containing the café, seen from the landside.

FEDERATION SQUARE

LEFT The new complex is designed to sit
above the railtracks, uniting downtown
Melbourne with the river.

This was the result of a competition won by
Lab Architecture Studio in a joint venture with
local firm Bates Smart. It was a breakthrough
commission for a practice with very little work
already built, but which styled itself 'a laboratory
of architectural speculation'.

The city of Melbourne developed with its
communication networks – the Yarra River and
railway station – side by side. This has meant that
the railway has historically limited access to the
north bank of the Yarra. The idea behind the
competition for Federation Square was to build
over the train tracks and link the central business
district with the riverbank while accommodating
a range of cultural facilities. When Lab won the
competition the brief included facilities for the
Australian Centre for the Moving Image (ACMI),
the SBS radio and television stations, offices and
retail, an exhibition gallery, an information area,
a performance space, and a civic square that
could accommodate 10,000 people. The biggest
post-competition change was the inclusion of
10,000 square metres (108,000 square feet) of
galleries to house the Australian art collection of
the National Gallery of Victoria (NGV).

The project began under a Liberal
government in Victoria but when Labor came to
power they directly influenced the course of the
scheme by scrapping plans for a 21-metre (69-
foot) high glass 'shard' at the northwestern corner
of the scheme. This had fallen foul of the heritage
lobby for blocking the view of the principal façade
of St Paul's Cathedral from the Princes Bridge.

FEDERATION SQUARE

OPPOSITE The street façade is made up of
layers of triangular panels.

FEDERATION SQUARE
OPPOSITE The Flinders Street elevation is
supported by a steel frame.

The 'shard' was to be replaced by a building no higher than 8 metres (26 feet). A huge row developed with broadly the heritage lobby on one side and the architectural lobby on the other. But the origins of the debate went back to the competition itself. When Lab won it was with a scheme that contradicted the competition brief by masking views of the cathedral from Princes Bridge. They had argued that the cathedral was too small a building to address such a large open space and should be enclosed with a smaller forecourt better related to its scale. This issue immediately became controversial, some critics arguing that: 'Whether or not this is valid is immaterial. The city has recently demolished the thirty-year-old Gas and Fuel Buildings expressly to reveal the cathedral. It makes no sense to block the view again.'[16]

Many people associated the protection of views of St Paul's with a respect for Melbourne's heritage. On the other hand supporting the scheme and saving the 'shard' came to be seen as progressive. A fact often quoted by the architectural press in praise of the building was that 150,000 people chose to gather here to denounce the Iraq war. This is a less remarkable acclamation of the design than it might seem, since providing a public meeting space had always been a key component of the competition brief. But it was assumed that since 150,000 Melbournians opposed the war, the same number also endorsed the building. In the end Premier Steve Backs used a report he commissioned from Professor Evan Walker to erase the northwest shard. This caused a lingering dispute, which has served to mask some of the most interesting questions that remain about the project.

Formal shapes dominate Federation Square. It is an agglomeration of acute triangles in plan, in section, and in the detailed composition of façades. Within these patterns, triangles are set within further triangles. The same types of shapes used in the site plan of the scheme appear on the façades of buildings. The architects described their design process in purely formal terms as a form of experimentation with shapes. Lab's abstract conceptual approach was certainly ambitious – at one point they explained: 'we have struggled to redraw the description of a line.'[17] Lab described their design process as involving the construction of 'a new ordering system' called 'Tectonic Aggregation'. This involves tracing patterns from photographs of geological strata and contemporary artwork before testing them 'against the particular circumstances of the project.'[18]

They recognized that whatever formal system they chose, it would have to distinguish between the different institutions contained in the site as well as provide an overall coherence. The façade system they developed to do this comprised three types of façades (or four including the shards). The buildings housing the ACMI, NGV, SBS studios and Yarra Building are made up of zinc, glass and sandstone from Donnybrook WA, used in different combinations. The X-bar building, by contrast, has a perforated zinc wall. The atrium is made from glass panels. The plaza and floor are clad in sandstone from the Kimberley region of WA.

Inside the square the advantages of the varied geometries became clear. They encourage variation in plan and section. The result is a picturesque urban piazza, assisted by the mix of functions within it, and entered by similarly interesting side streets. The external façades are less successful. These provide Federation Square with a public face made up of fractal geometries that feel overworked. It is a system without any economy of means, almost as if the intention were complexity for complexity's sake. Part of the problem with these fractal geometries is that they do not relate to any credible scale or proportion other than to themselves. Also disappointing is the way the buildings screen the river, especially considering that a key intention of the competition was to encourage access to it.

Some critics have interpreted this use of a tight compositional palette of repeated triangular forms as a direct response to the prevailing zeitgeist. Charles Jencks, when describing the scheme, pointed to what he believed was a 'deep transformation occurring in the sciences.' For Jencks, Federation Square reflected, 'new sciences of complexity – fractals, nonlinear dynamics, the new cosmology, self-

organizing systems…. Illuminated by the
computer this new worldview is paralleled
by transformations now occurring in
architecture'.[19] He saw this building as 'a seminal
work of the new movement'. The formal use of
triangular shapes to make up this composition
are, for Jencks, examples of 'the new paradigm'[20]
affecting all scientific and artistic activities on
the planet. The central assumption behind this
interpretation of the zeitgeist is that since
'fractals' are recent products of science then
architecture, if it is to remain 'modern', must
incorporate them as literal visual motifs.
There may be no direct logical explanation for
the employment of specific triangular shapes
to clad buildings or to determine their floor
plans but what seems to matter for Jencks is
that they are triangular (and therefore 'fractal')
and they result in an architecture that looks
complicated (because the new science is
complicated).

Certainly the application of a gratuitously
complex visual vocabulary has enormous
benefits for the media interest an architectural
practice receives, and Federation Square looks
strikingly unlike the much more economically
clad buildings in the rest of the city. A book
produced to accompany the opening of the
scheme attempts to explain Lab's obsessive use
of triangular shapes: 'Fractured geometry
represents the order of our times. It takes the
mathematical theories and diagrams of the
Penroses and uses them as disordering devices

for planning architecture. In this chaotic order
we can wander without need for visual clues to
guide our path, things are not apparent, and do
not occur where they maybe should be.'[21] The
coded message is: 'don't worry if you can't
understand this building, you're not supposed to
unless you're clever enough to understand very
complex mathematics.' Davidson, looking back
at the completed Federation Square declared
that: 'it arrived from outer space but looks like it
belongs.' What is certain is that Jencks and the
architects expected this convoluted visual
grammar to be interpreted as both profound and
technologically advanced.

To borrow Chermayeff's phrase, the
'shapemakers' are back. But they are not just
presenting intellectual or artistic statement
architecture. They are couching their statements
in something that has to look the way it does
because it is at the technological forefront.
Libeskind's 'shards' are actually much less
expressive of the destructive forces of war
and loss than they are of the complexity and
precision of some more technologically
advanced civilization, as if 'arrived from outer
space'. Gehry's curves do not appear to us
gratuitous sculptural gestures, because of their
aircraft-software moulded titanium hide.

What about the 'problem-solvers'
themselves? A number of the architects who
made their names with buildings of great
formal simplicity now produce buildings of
considerable formal complexity when

approached with an arts complex brief. Even
Norman Foster.

In 2004 Foster and Partners built the **Sage**
music complex for the North Music Trust at
Gateshead on the south bank of the River Tyne.
The North Music Trust comprises three
organizations: the Northern Sinfonia chamber
orchestra, the Folkworks folk music
development agency and the Sage Music
Education Centre. The name 'Sage' itself derives
from the sponsorship provided by a local
software company. The building follows a simple
diagram, with three auditoriums built in a row.
For acoustic reasons they are built entirely
apart, and to ensure even greater acoustic
separation another roof structure sails over
them all. Its shape loosely shrink-wraps the
auditoria below leaving a large amount of
circulation and foyer space.

The first auditorium (seating 1,700) follows
the classic 'shoe-box' design which until recently
had fallen out of favour with auditorium
designers who tended towards wider shell-plan
schemes. It is expressly designed to
accommodate the Northern Sinfonia whose
musical repertoire is best served acoustically
by a hall of this type. The interior is clad in
American white ash installed by specialist
joinery contractor Abrahams & Carlisle. Arup
Acoustics acted as acoustician and with Foster
and Partners devised a system that allows
panels in the ceiling to be adjusted to suit the
size of the orchestra. Sound can be absorbed by

moving motorized curtains across 90 per cent of the wall area. The second auditorium, seating 400, is designed for a chamber repertoire but with the flexibility to allow for modern genres such as folk, jazz and electronic music. The walls within its decagon form were designed with a bow-shaped profile to assist in sound diffusion. The final smaller shoebox hall, the Northern Rock Foundation Hall, is primarily designed as the rehearsal space for the Northern Sinfonia

and consequently reflects the acoustic characteristics of the main hall. It also serves as a venue for chamber music, solos and other smaller scale performances.

Unlike many buildings by Foster and Partners, the Sage did not receive universally positive reviews. Ellis Woodman regretted that 'the Sage's shed-like composition results in some all too predictable disappointments.'[22] He mentioned the disjunction at either end of the

building where sheer glass elevations are equipped with very small doors set in very large walls. He complains that despite some variation the roof is essentially a continuation of Foster's extruded shapes which date all the way back to the Sainsbury Centre. It is a building that fails to enclose the space of the harbour. Instead it is simply a large gestural shape that sits within the space of the harbour: 'A building without parts. A building of a single, unmodulated scale

A building without top or bottom, without front or back.'[23]

Woodman was one of several to criticize the Sage's scale-less quality. The critics were not suggesting that it simply dwarfs surrounding structures but that the single oversailing roof fails to provide any human scale that relates to its location. In this regard the Hilton Hotel by the Tyne Bridge in Gateshead makes a useful comparison. This is a similarly large building, whose only indication of scale are the little square windows that indicate its floor levels and these only emphasize how big it is. But unlike the dismal architecture of this hotel the Sage's curved form draws attention to itself yet at the same time fails to create attractive public spaces around it. For Woodman it was not the sheer size of the Sage that was at fault (indeed the even larger Baltic Exchange building was praised in comparison) but its outer shell. He suggested that had the Sage's large-span roof been omitted it might reveal a far more successful urban presence beneath.

The Sage has disappointed critics who prefer buildings that create public spaces around them rather than forming a detached, if striking, shape. But the Sage can also be criticized on its own terms. The slick cladding and complex form, a smooth conjunction of interlocked toroids, gives its exterior a sense of great technical virtuosity. However, seen from the inside the slick skin is revealed as being supported by a skeletal structure of very familiar building components, such as I-beams. It disappoints, if only because the exterior seemed to promise more. This sense is reinforced at night when the interior is lit through a number of clear panels creating a

'pixilation' effect rather than following any purely designed shape.

The partner in charge of the project, Spenser de Grey, justifies the form of the Sage through the efficiency it achieves in terms of floor to external wall ratio, and the quality of its cladding.[24] Certainly the Sage was built on a remarkably limited budget for such a large building that contains a range of impressive auditoria and all their ancillary functions. De Grey saw nothing wrong with its simple diagram. As far as De Grey was concerned, they had answered a complex cultural brief with a simple engineering-led solution, just like the widely acclaimed Sainsbury Centre built almost thirty years before. But these disparate views suggested that architects and critics were talking at cross-purposes, as if Foster and Partners had, in designing the Sage, crossed a

line that some of the architectural press were unwilling to follow.

Architect Jean Nouvel also used an oversailing canopy to cover the range of different venues demanded by a predominantly classical music centre. Nouvel, like Foster, has built a number of very high profile projects but they are not as easily recognizable. Nouvel is very open about the fact that he draws very little and approaches projects in an entirely analytical fashion,[25] developing buildings in a 'design process…as much verbal as visual.'[26]

The **Cultural and Conference Centre Lucerne (KKL)** is a project that dates back to 1989 when Nouvel won an invited competition for a new concert hall to house the famous International Music Festival. Like so many arts complexes, included in the brief were an additional 900-seat multi-purpose hall, a 300-seat conference

CULTURAL AND CONFERENCE CENTRE LUCERNE (KKL)
ABOVE A single horizontal plane oversails the entire scheme.

CULTURAL AND CONFERENCE CENTRE LUCERNE (KKL)
OPPOSITE The lake flows in narrow channels between the elements of the design.

CULTURAL AND CONFERENCE
CENTRE LUCERNE (KKL)
BELOW The top floor opens up into a terrace
below the oversailing roof. The top of
the auditorium penetrates the space
within a curved wooden cladding.

CULTURAL AND CONFERENCE
CENTRE LUCERNE (KKL)
OPPOSITE The north-facing foyers overlook the lake.

auditorium and an art museum. Nouvel's competition scheme proposed housing the concert hall in a building that stuck out into the lake of Lucerne in an explicitly shiplike form. The old Kunsthaus building would remain but would be linked to the rest of the scheme by an oversailing canopy. However, this proposal fell foul of planning because of its intervention into the lake. After a protracted process Nouvel was asked to submit a revised scheme, which removed the old building but respected the existing water's edge. This was put to the popular vote again and this time won. The result is a project that has pulled back from the lake but has brought the lake forward via channels into the building.

Like the Sage it houses various independent elements that benefit acoustically from being separated under a single roof. But its roof serves solely as a canopy, providing the scheme as a visual datum, its flatness echoing the surface of the water. It sails out over the lake, its corner supported by a 45-metre (148-foot) cantilever. Within the building the canopy serves to frame the city all around it and from the city it locates the scheme in the landscape.

At the back of the building are service roads and facilities and then a line of administrative offices that shield the lakeside from the city. Here three auditoria, a concert hall, a multi-function hall and a congress hall sit in a row beneath the canopy separated by stretches of water. They are entered from the

timber walkway that runs along the water's edge. The main concert hall auditorium juts into the foyer. Clad in maple plywood, its shape echoes the curves both of a ship and of an enormous musical instrument. Working with Russell Johnson of acousticians Artec, Nouvel designed a classic 'shoe-box' proportioned chamber whose height is accommodated by digging down to first basement level. Nouvel successfully lobbied to reduce the number of

seats from the proposed 2,000 to 1,840, to ensure that overwhelming numbers did not form too much of a an acoustic sponge. Elements in the ceiling are lowered for chamber concerts, and curtains are pulled across the surrounding walls for electronic music events.

Both the Sage and the KKL deal with the issue of locating three distinct volumes in a single building form. The Sage was conceived as a solution to the technical problems of enclosing

CULTURAL AND CONFERENCE
CENTRE LUCERNE (KKL)
PREVIOUS SPREAD The primary auditorium.

CULTURAL AND CONFERENCE
CENTRE LUCERNE (KKL)
LEFT The KKL seen across the lake of Lucerne.
The flatness of the underside of the roof
echoes the flatness of the water.

breakout spaces and the provision of an efficient weatherproofing cover to the whole. It has an extremely efficient floor-to-cladding ratio and its aerodynamic shape channels the prevailing southwesterly wind providing natural ventilation to the concourse and education centre. Perhaps this building's mixed critical reception reflects the explicit, almost shameless, nature of Foster and Partners' diagrammatic thinking. Certainly it was not the only brief that they tackled in this fashion. Their Free University of Berlin has similar 1930s-inspired internal buildings with solid white balustrades looking out over a space, all oversailed by an enormous independent canopy. Foster and Partners perfected this technique over twenty years, completely differentiating a building's cladding from its internal configuration. In this sense the independent oversailing canopies of the Sage and Free University can be seen as inheritors of Buckminster Fuller's vision of covering the whole of Manhattan with a single roof. The problem with the Sage was simply that here they failed to convince everyone that traditional virtues such as the provision of a decent urban face, or the creation of public spaces around the building were also resolved by the large-span gesture. The seamless shrink-wrapped solution to both buildings' briefs is perhaps perceived as being rather too convenient.

In Lucerne, Architectures Jean Nouvel, by choosing to open all three buildings to the elements, make it clear that the canopy's primary function is a deliberate formal gesture that knits the building into the cityscape and responds to the horizontal plane of the lake. Nouvel, while very much a problem-solving architect, in this project recognizes 'urban presence' as an element in his equation.

Most of the new arts centres feature large volumes defined by highly engineered technological skins. But in some ways the skins of these buildings are not technologically that remarkable. Curved surfaces only become structural if they enable the development of efficient membrane stresses allowing thin surfaces to carry substantial loads. Look behind the cladding of Disney and Sage and you find that they are not themselves load bearing but are supported by skeletons of conventional steel members. Skeleton structures actually carry a great deal of load using bending stresses — one of the least efficient methods of support. Compared to the greatly efficient concrete shell structures of the 20th century such as the work of, say, Félix Candela, the new arts sheds are not that efficient.[27] But like the Sydney Opera House, which is actually supported by very inefficient heavy ribs, it is the appearance of technical virtuosity that counts.

INFLUENCE

INFLUENCE
The Spread of the Shed

In the past architects could look at ancient cathedrals, temples and pyramids and believe themselves to be the authors of equally 'permanent' monuments. Today, however, few architects are sustained by this myth, in large part because the building industry has changed completely. Obsolescence is one of the central features of modern life. Contemporary steel structures are rarely designed to last more than one hundred years and their complex servicing rarely lasts longer than thirty.

One logical response to architecture's newly found impermanence has been to view it not as a problem but as an asset. Perhaps the transience of architecture should be embraced. Would it not make sense to design buildings with all the advantages of the latest technology, which could then be replaced by superior versions when they are invented? As we saw in 'Origins' (pp. 16–35), this approach was first recommended by the inventor Buckminster Fuller and articulated by critic Reyner Banham. They encouraged architects to build impermanent structures that used contemporary industrial processes and embraced future change. Buildings should be flexible, allowing for future manipulation by their occupants as their needs change and as building technologies improve. The easiest way to accommodate these requirements was to create a neutral volume of space, serviced from its periphery. During the 1970s a number of architects including Kisho Kurokawa, Norman Foster, Richard Rogers and Renzo Piano explored this idea. Their buildings were not designed to last forever: Richard Rogers is said confidently to have asserted before the Pompidou Centre was complete that he and Piano were building for just thirty years. Yet these buildings were designed to provide their occupants with enormous flexibility. This was what was radical about the Pompidou and Sainsbury Centres, not the smooth aluminium skins or rows of coloured ducts that inspired the title 'High-Tech'.

As we have seen, sheds were not simply invented by dreamers like Archigram and architects like Foster but follow the development of new building types during the Industrial Revolution. Factories and exhibition buildings always required simple open spaces and large spans. But the specific importance of buildings like the Pompidou and Sainsbury Centres lay in the careers of those who designed them. Piano, Rogers and Foster went on to become dominant figures in their profession. Whether their early buildings really were flexible or provided neutral space, the ideas they chose to explore became very influential.

More recently the technologist approach of Piano and Foster appears to have been challenged by the work of self-consciously art-based architects. Frank Gehry and Daniel Libeskind build in signature styles seemingly derived from their own individual artistic visions. Yet they bound their ideas in technological wrappers and so their buildings are not only distinctive but also futuristic. Rather than rejecting the technological shed they have customized it, and made it take original forms.

Today, while sheds have become commonplace, many of the ideas that accompanied their ideological birth have not yet reached maturity. One idea popular in the 1960s and 1970s was that of literal flexibility – the ability of buildings to move. Airports are routinely designed to allude to the idea of flight, or resemble aeroplanes or birds but they remain static. Industrial buildings have pods on legs but they can't actually walk. Renzo Piano reflected on his Pompidou building that: 'Our friends Archigram and Cedric Price are right it's not very dynamic.'[1] Since then hydraulics have enabled bridges and sections of cladding to move but we are scarcely any closer to Archigram's vision of Walking Cities. At the time a primary aspiration was to create something mechanical rather than architectural. Critic Peter Blake remarked that with Archigram suddenly 'everything was architecture', inspired by a vision of architecture as not necessarily being about buildings. Instead, it could involve space suits and inflatable structures, rather than piles of masonry.

The dowdy child of all this visionary enthusiasm was the neutral serviced space, the generic shed. This has become a fundamental building type, much less exciting than many other ideas from the 1960s but no less important. For the type of buildings we have explored in detail form only the visible tip of a

SENDAI MEDIATHEQUE

RIGHT Patterns of translucent rectangles
partially screen the sun and act as
spandrel panels obscuring the edges
of the slabs.

SENDAI MEDIATHEQUE

FOLLOWING SPREAD Ito's double-layered glass façade acts as
a thermal chimney. In summer, veils at
the top allow for the rapid release of
heat; in winter, they close to form a
thermal blanket.

much larger, if less distinguished, iceberg.
Moreover, their influence can also be seen in the
design of buildings that are only in some senses
sheds. Some are buildings influenced by large-
span and large-volume building solutions, while
others explore the shed aesthetic. A unique
example of a large-span building is Toyo Ito's
Mediatheque in Sendai, an industrial city 350
kilometres (220 miles) northeast of Tokyo. At
first sight the Mediatheque looks like a very
familiar 'Domino'-inspired[2] building, a cube with
very clearly defined floor plates. But on closer
inspection, each storey is found to be of
different height. Each has a different ceiling
finish, is furnished in a different way and is lit in
a different manner. And while the building's boxy
shape eschews any association with large-span
architecture, the floor plates are supported not
by an orderly 'Domino' alignment of columns
but by thirteen steel latticework cages that run
between them. This radical scheme reflects Toyo
Ito's abstract competition model of 1994 in
which he presented his idea of thirteen 'tubes'
supporting open-plan 'plates' surrounded by a
glazed cladding (or 'skin'). Between then and the
Mediatheque's completion in 2000 the
programme determining the building's contents
was constantly reviewed in protracted political
discussions between rival authorities in Sendai.
So while in Tokyo Toyo Ito was designing the
building, in Sendai its intended function
continued to change until a year before
completion. Ito had to create a diagram simple

PHOENIX CENTRAL LIBRARY

RIGHT The building was planned on a 9.96-metre
(32-foot) square grid – dimensions based
on a standard library stack.

PHOENIX CENTRAL LIBRARY

FOLLOWING SPREAD The lightweight shed-like character
of the reading room is emphasized
by the steel roof that visually 'hovers'
above the columns.

and flexible enough to accommodate a shifting brief – following the ideal of flexibility championed by Archigram and first attempted at the Pompidou Centre.

Ito's 'plates' were envisaged as very thin flat slabs. Usually these would be made of reinforced concrete, but to span the required 20 metres (66 feet) would need a 700-millimetre (28-inch) thick slab. The structural engineer, Mutsuro Sasaki, recognized that the slabs had to be much lighter as their combined dead load would necessitate a different structural system. The solution was to make the floor plates from two thin steel surfaces sandwiching steel ribs. These ribs spread out in radial patterns around the latticework cages, the distance between them varying over the plan in response to the changing patterns of load. Each steel sandwich is a remarkably thin 400 millimetres (16 inches), with a 70-millimetre ($2^3/_4$-inch) lightweight screed on top. Their hollow cores also allow them to act as a plenum allowing conditioned air to be distributed around the plan.

The 'trees' (latticework steel cages) are composed of steel tubes of varying diameter (120–240 millimetres/$4^3/_4$–$9^1/_2$ inches) and thickness (10–30 millimetres/$5/_6$–$1^1/_4$ inches) depending upon their location. They are fixed to the foundations and pin-jointed to the slabs. As they primarily absorb compression and bending stresses, which increase lower down, their cross-sections swell towards the ground. The cages hold a variety of functions. The largest contain

the building's circulation with lifts and staircases. The smallest in the centre of the plan are light-wells. Above them, on the roof, computer-controlled sun reflectors automatically tilt and turn to funnel in light. The four corner cages are the widest, with a triangular profile of lattice that acts as a truss in order to counteract wind loads and the effects of earthquakes. The result is an extraordinarily open plan of 2,500 square metres (27,000 square feet) on each floor, only divided by temporary screens and furniture. These contain the Sendai Public Library, the Sendai Civic Art Gallery, the Sendai Audiovisual Learning Centre and a centre for people with disabilities. The Mediatheque is really a big public library with some additional features. Yet some of its details reinforce the idea that it provides an innovative 'media' experience. The south façade, the main public face of the building overlooking Jozenji Street, is made of two layers of glass. In the winter the space between them is closed off to act as a glazed thermal blanket. In the summer it is vented at the top to act as a thermal chimney drawing off hot air. Direct sun is partially shielded by patterns of translucent rectangles that diffuse light into the plan, which also serve as spandrel-panels obscuring the edge of the floor plates when seen from outside. Their distinct repetitious nature and 'mechanical' shape also suggest that they satisfy Ito's well-known fascination with bar codes and other computer-read imagery. Ultimately, the simple

container and diagrammatic design reveal a self-conscious determination to make the 'mediatheque' a new building typology. The scope of Ito's ambitions for the project are revealed in an explanation given to *GA Document 66*: 'Mediatheque…would offer itself as a place where the body as an electronic fluid and the primitive body united with nature integrate into one.' It is strange that structurally so extraordinary a shed is designed to resemble a standard office building.

The **Phoenix Central Library**, by contrast, rejects its Domino frame and while structurally an 'office' is visually a shed. Designed by Will Bruder (in collaboration with DWL Architects)

the library wholly embraces a large-span aesthetic. Phoenix Central Library had outgrown its existing facility and wanted a new building large enough to allow for expansion. With limited resources the city authorities required a 22,300 square metre (240,000 square foot) building for a budget of $28 million (£20 million). The new library supplies 26,000 square metres (280,000 square feet) for the original budget, at a remarkable US$100 per square foot. This was achieved by using the sort of basic concrete frame system that typically supports multi-storey warehouses – buildings similarly required to store heavy things cheaply. The precast frame, a double-T system over

dropped girders, supports massive 90- by 60-metre (295- by 197-foot) floor plates. The 'T's have 760-millimetre (30-inch) downstands which, as well as providing enough structural depth for the load of the books, leave space for a service zone.

Two service wings with dense concrete walls stand on the east and west sides of the building providing lateral restraint for the frame. These wings hold the service lifts, emergency exit stairs and toilets, as well as mechanical and electrical plant, and provide thermal insulation to the books within. Corrugated copper panel cladding emphasizes their visual mass, recalling the silos and barns of the Arizonan landscape.

PHOENIX CENTRAL LIBRARY
ABOVE The library has an aesthetic derived from buildings such as silos, found in the open landscape of Arizona.

PHOENIX CENTRAL LIBRARY
OPPOSITE Above each entrance the copper façade is pulled back to reveal a layer of stainless steel – an idea inspired by the rock strata of the Arizona desert.

PHOENIX CENTRAL LIBRARY
FOLLOWING SPREAD Rejecting the 'Domino' frame of the towers of downtown Phoenix, the library instead shows off the uninterrupted span.

This is no accident as the copper was moulded by a machine that makes cladding for grain silos. Bruder further emphasized the Western metaphor by describing the wings as 'saddlebags'. On the first four floors the structural system dictates the internal character of the spaces and a rather banal series of library stacks are only enlivened by views out of the north and south glazed walls. However, visitors arriving at the non-fiction department on the fifth floor find themselves in a huge spacious room. Here the tapered columns extend the grid from the lower floors but stop tantalizingly close to the ceiling where a lightwell sits above each. A network of diagonal interlocking cable trusses,

running from a crown near the summit of each column, supports a tubular steel purlin system that holds a metal roof.

Bruder claims the form of the building derives from what he refers to as his 'functional metaphors'. The curved copper walls of the 'saddle-bags' with their horizontal striations are said to be inspired by the mesa of Monument Valley. Above each entrance the copper is peeled back to reveal stainless steel like a second rock stratum exposed by denudation. Other metaphors also suggest themselves such as railway carriages or farm buildings. All these readings assist Bruder in his attempt to provide a clear visual language at odds with the building's

concrete frame. His form suggests, instead, two
solid elements that flank a wide open space.
But this achieves its full expression only where
the columns on the fifth floor do not meet the
lightweight roof but act more like the poles of a
tent and seem to tether it. Bruder was forced to
build a concrete frame building but inspired by
rock formations and the functionalist tradition of
the American West has visualized it as a shed.

Bruder's particular shed-aesthetic is one
derived from the agricultural buildings of the
American West. The influence of local pre-
existing sheds upon a new design is not unique.
It can be seen working in the very different
context of a London hinterland at Herzog and
de Meuron's **Laban**. The Laban Centre for
Movement and Dance is a contemporary dance
school originally founded by Rudolf Laban in
1948. Its new building is located in an area of low
industrial buildings next to Deptford Creek –
a tidal tributary of the Thames. Herzog and
de Meuron clearly took inspiration from the low-
cost industrial context, and built an inexpensive
low-slung box. This is orientated around a curved
entrance wall whose geometry responds to
St Paul's church (1712–30), a rare monument in
an area dominated by relatively impermanent
buildings.

Central to this manipulation of the
lightweight box aesthetic was the building's
innovative cladding. This consists of a sandwich
of elements. Coloured, transparent polycarbonate

The polycarbonate contributes to the thermal performance of the exterior skin but also gives it visual depth and complexity. A range of three colours – turquoise, green and magenta – was added to the inner leaf of the polycarbonate during extrusion, and these project onto the white walls behind to create a shimmering effect.

The polycarbonate panels are laid flush without visible fixings and contain occasional rectangles of glass. These reflect the surroundings during the day and open up clearer views into the building at night. At the same time clear glass appears behind the polycarbonate at night revealing blurred profiles of the dancers. Sharp images and delicate impressions combine in visual layers of clarity. As architect Tim Ronalds, writing in *Architecture*

LABAN
PREVIOUS SPREAD The dance studios are entirely surrounded by translucent cladding.

LABAN
OPPOSITE The entrance façade is curved in the direction of St Paul's church – a rare masonry monument among a sea of lightweight buildings.

LABAN
ABOVE The entrance corridor lies perpendicular to the front façade.

LABAN
FOLLOWING SPREAD The building is entered through a small, undistinguished door.

CITY OF ARTS AND SCIENCES

RIGHT While Calatrava's concrete structures
can be seen as part of a separate
tradition of Eero Saarinen and Pier
Luigi Nervi, the spaces chosen for the
City of Arts and Sciences are neutral
volumes under grand spans.

CITY OF ARTS AND SCIENCES

FOLLOWING SPREAD 'Flying buttresses' are used on a
gigantic scale.

Today summarized, it is: 'An ethereal magical
shed among the other sheds around Deptford
Creek; of its place, but not.'[3]

Sheds have had a far more subtle influence
than might at first be apparent. The career of the
famous Spanish architect Santiago Calatrava
might appear to be free of the influence of the
big shed. Calatrava trained as an architect in his
native Valencia and then as an engineer at the
ETH in Zurich. His 1981 thesis 'Concerning the
Foldability of Space Frames' led to a lifelong
fascination with moving structures that has
dominated his career. Resisting the rush to build
in steel and follow a technological aesthetic he
has built predominantly in concrete following
the alternative tradition of Kenzo Tange, Pier
Luigi Nervi and Eero Saarinen. His recent
projects have been very deliberately world-class
iconic buildings, a genre Deyan Sudjic aptly
defines as: 'a cultural building, designed with a
heavy subsidy from public funds, with the
express purpose of getting previously obscure
cities into the pages of inflight magazines.'[4]
Calatrava's masterpiece, the £2 billion **City of
Arts and Sciences**, was built in his hometown,
Valencia. While its striking concrete and steel
structures catch the eye it is easy to overlook a
fundamental characteristic of these buildings.
Calatrava's brief was incredibly loose. He was
able to build pretty much anything he wanted,
yet chose a structure that maximized the
impression of a huge volume. The Science
Museum, the largest structure on the site,

is 241 metres (791 feet) long and 104 metres (341 feet) wide. It was designed as a great cathedral of space replete with a new kind of flying buttress. Whether or not it resembles a new form of gothic or a 'bleached skeleton of a long-dead sea creature, inflated to a giant scale',[5] it is a huge large-volume structure. Calatrava's buildings might not technically be described as sheds, since they are built as permanent monuments in concrete, but his decision to use a large-span and large-volume structure when attempting a sort of ultimate icon indicates their prevailing influence over architects seeking the maximum dramatic impact.

Many of today's seminal structures have more in common with lightweight industrial units than they do with the famous masonry buildings that will precede them in the history books. This is not necessarily a pejorative evaluation – it simply reflects the degree to which architecture was changed by the 20th century. The rise of the big shed reflects both the changing economics of the building industry and the decision of designers and architects to help change it. This process has not been inevitable. The architects who developed it had, at the time, a clear idea of what satisfied their particular zeitgeist, and many clients in turn found their conclusions satisfying. These innovators sought diagrammatic solutions to problems in the same practical engineered way that Paxton solved the

logistical problem of the Great Exhibition. In doing so they set a fundamental idea in place: that however idiosyncratic a building is, it is more convincing when it resembles a by-product of technical innovation. The shed form was thus not driven directly by technology but by the way architects responded to the idea of 'technology', and how seriously we, in turn, took the products of their response.

The question remains why the idea of technology has proved so consistently popular? Perhaps as laymen we are happier with an unashamedly new-looking object when it is clearly a product of science – one that suggests 'it looks this way in order to work'. We are less sanguine if the shape of an object appears to reflect a designer's gratuitous choice, especially if it contradicts our current preference. A white modernist house could obviously have been built differently had its designer chosen to do so. A modern airport, on the other hand, has to look the way it does in order to work, or so we assume. We judge it with the same bemused optimism we apply to the aircraft, because we cannot divorce our view of its appearance from its practical attributes. Aeroplanes have moulded forms and wide wings but it is their miraculous capacity to fly that encourages us to see these machines as beautiful. And since we are about to be transported across continents we are in no position to judge their appearance objectively. The best big sheds follow the same magic formula.

NOTES

PREFACE (p. 8)

1 Critic Martin Pawley was one of the first to codify them as a significant phenomenon. He suggested in his book *Terminal Architecture* (1998) that 'Big Sheds, can be found all over the British Isles, everywhere except in the centre of our towns and cities…'. He stated that up to a third of all new serviced floorspace was built in them.

2 H. Pearman, *Airports: A Century of Architecture*, Laurence King, 2004, p. 14

3 Ibid., p. 14

ORIGINS (pp. 16–35)

1 Quoted in H. C. Sculitz, *Industrial Building: The Future of Tradition*, p. 21

2 J. Ruskin, *The Seven Lamps of Architecture*, George Allen, 1886, p. 40

3 S. Giedion, *Space, Time and Architecture*, Harvard University Press, 1949, p. 146

4 Ibid., p. 151

5 N. Pevsner, *Pioneers of the Modern Movement*, London, 1936, p. 202

6 For Pevsner, 'expressionism was a short interlude, following early Gropius and preceding the mature Gropius of the Bauhaus building at Dessau…'. See N. Pevsner, *Pioneers of Modern Design* (3rd edn), London, 1974, p. 217

7 This phrase was added to the last chapter of later editions. See N. Pevsner, *Pioneers of Modern Design*, Yale, 2005, p. 163

8 As Pevsner put it, 'architects as well as clients must know that today's reality, exactly as that of 1914, can find its complete expression only in the style created by the giants of that by now distant past…. The whims of individual architects, the strokes of genius of others cannot be accepted as an answer to the serious questions which it is the responsibility of the architect to answer.' See N. Pevsner, *Pioneers of Modern Design* (3rd edn), London, 1974, p. 217

9 R. Banham, 'Revenge of the Picturesque: English Architectural Polemics 1945–1965', in J. Summerson (ed.), *Concerning Architecture: Essays on architectural writers and writing presented to Nikolaus Pevsner*, Allen Lane, 1968

10 N. Whiteley, *Reyner Banham: Historian of the Immediate Future*, MIT Press, 2002, p. 39

11 R. Banham, 'Machine Aesthetic', in *Architectural Association*, April, 1955, p. 226

12 R. Banham, 'Le Corbusier', in *New Society*, 14 September 1967, p. 354

13 R. Buckminster Fuller, 'Influences on My Work' (1955) in J. Meller (ed.), *The Buckminster Fuller Reader*, London, 1972, p. 64

14 See M. Pawley, *Buckminster Fuller*, Grafton, 1992

15 P. Johnson, 'Where We Are At', in *Architectural Review*, September 1960, p. 175

16 R. Banham, *The New Brutalism: Ethic or aesthetic*, Architectural Press, 1966

17 On 20 July 1957 Harold Macmillan addressed a Conservative Party rally at Bedford with the words: 'Indeed let us be frank about it: most of our people have never had it so good…. Go around the country, go to the industrial towns, go to the farms, and you will see a state of prosperity such as we have never had in my lifetime – nor indeed in the history of this country.'

18 *Archigram*, television programme, directed by Archigram, BBC Productions, 1966

19 Quoted in M. Emanuel (ed.), *Contemporary Architects*, London, 1980

20 Richard Rogers in D. Jenkins (ed.), *On Foster… Foster On*, Prestel, 2000, p. 271

21 A. Colquhoun, *Essays in Architectural Criticism: Modern Architecture and Historical Change*, MIT Press, 1981, pp. 112–17

22 Quoted in N. Silver, *The Making of Beaubourg: A building biography of the Centre Pompidou, Paris*, MIT Press, 1994, p. 185

23 Hilton Kramer in *The New York Times*, 30 Jan 1977. Quoted in B. Appleyard, *Richard Rogers: A Biography*, London, 1986, p. 221

24 Mark Stevens in *Newsweek*, 2 January 1978. Quoted in B. Appleyard, *Richard Rogers: A Biography*, London, 1986, p. 221

25 M. Spring in *Building Week*, 7 April 1978, p. 52

26 Lucinda Hawkins in *Art Monthly*, no. 17, June 1978, p. 27

27 Editorial in *The Burlington Magazine*, no. 906, vol. CXX, Sept. 1978, p. 565

28 Sutherland Lyall in *New Society*, 6 July 1978, p. 26

29 See N. Foster, 'Richard Buckminster Fuller' in T. T. K. Zung (ed.), *Buckminster Fuller: Anthology for the New Millennium*, New York, 2001, p. 4

30 Andrew Peckham in *AD Special Issue*, vol. 49, no. 2, 1979

31 Peter Cook in *Architectural Review*, December 1978, p. 356

EXHIBITION (pp. 36–83)

1 Quoted in L. Benevolo, *History of Modern Architecture* (vol. 1), London, 1971, p. 101

2 Quoted in A. Trachtenberg, *The Incorporation of America: Culture and Society in the Gilded Age*, Hill & Wang, 1982, p. 215

3 According to Mary Pepchinski in *Architectural Record*, July 2000, p. 30

4 These organizations include the Fraunhofer Association, Technical University of Munich and Centre for applied Energy Research of Bavaria

5 *The Observer*, 30 Jan. 2000

6 C. Amery, 'Architecture of Nick Grimshaw' in *Nicholas Grimshaw and Partners: Book 2: Process*, published by Nicholas Grimshaw and Partners, p. 8

7 N. Grimshaw, 'Autobiographical Note' in *Nicholas Grimshaw and Partners: Book 2: Process*, published by Nicholas Grimshaw and Partners, p. 13

8 Quoted in N. Grimshaw 'Autobiographical Note' in *Nicholas Grimshaw and Partners: Book 2: Process*, published by Nicholas Grimshaw and Partners, p. 19

9 K. Powell, Introduction in R. Moore, (ed.), *Structure, Space & Skin*, London, 1993, p. 10

10 C. Amery, *Architecture, Industry and Innovation: The Early Work of Nicholas Grimshaw & Partners*, London, 1995, pp. 10–11

11 Peter Davey in *Architectural Review*, August 2001, p. 31

12 Quoted in Deborah K. Dietsch, 'Urban Nexus', in *Architecture* (AIA), October 1996, p. 115

13 See S. Lyall, *Remarkable Structures: Engineering Today's Innovative Buildings*, Princeton Architectural Press, 2002, p. 84

14 Quoted in R.A.B., 'Glass Hall', in *Architecture* (AIA), October 1996, p. 132

INDUSTRY (pp. 84–113)

1 SIAT Architektur + Technik, *CK21: The Cargolifter Shipyard*, Munich, 2001

2 Ibid., p. 34

TRANSPORT (pp. 114–87)

1 In an interview with Jonathan Glancey broadcast on BBC Radio 3 at 6.30pm on 2 June 1989, published in C. Amery, *Architecture, Industry and Innovation: The Early Work of Nicholas Grimshaw & Partners*, London, 1995, p. 247

2 H. Pearman, *Contemporary World Architecture*, London, 2002, p. 360. He expresses similar views in *Airports: A century of architecture*, London, 2004

3   Quoted in 'Kansai International Airport Passenger Terminal Building; Architects Renzo Piano and Building Workshop', *Japan Architect*, no. 15 (3), Autumn 1996, pp. 2–24

4   Quoted in 'Good Korea Move; Architects Terry Farrell & Partners', in *Building Design*, no. 1515, 11 Jan. 2002, p. 11

5   Quoted by D. Cohn in *Architectural Record*, Oct. 2005, p. 150

6   Quoted by N. A. Solomon in *Architectural Record*, Oct. 2005, p. 182

SPORT (pp. 188–211)

1   S. Kuper, 'EURO 2004: The view from the home stand isn't very good', in *Financial Times*, 19 June 2004

2   Quoted in M. Payne, *Olympic Turnaround: How the Olympic Games stepped back from the brink of extinction to become the world's best known brand – and a multi-billion dollar global franchise*, London, 2005, p. 184

3   Ibid., p. 185

4   Quoted in P. Stürzebecher and S. Ulrich, *Architecture for Sport: New Concepts and International Projects for Sport and Leisure*, London, 2002, p. 128

ARTS (pp. 212–61)

1   N. Pevsner, *Pioneers of Modern Design* (3rd edn), London, 1974, p. 217

2   J. Zulaika, *Guggenheim Bilbao Museoa: Museums, Architecture, and City Renewal*, Centre for Basque Studies, University of Nevada, Reno, 2003, p. 113

3   V. Newhouse, *Towards a New Museum*, New York, 1998, p. 191

4   D. Sudjic, *The Edifice Complex*, London, 2005, p. 278

5   *A&U*, no. 1 (400), January 2004, p. 14

6   H. Muschamp, *The New York Times Magazine*, 7 Sept. 1997, pp. 54–9, 72, 82

7   G. Joseph, 'Frank Gehry, public artist' in *Art in America*, Nov. 2004

8   Ibid.

9   W. J. Mitchell in 'Roll Over Euclid: How Frank Gehry Designs and Builds' in J. F. Ragheb (ed.), *Frank Gehry Architect*, Guggenheim Museum, 2001, pp. 356–7

10   S. Lyall, *Remarkable Structures: Engineering Today's Innovative Buildings*, Princeton, 2002, p. 150

11   *Architectural Record*, no. 1, 1999, p. 84

12   D. Libeskind and B. Schneider, *Daniel Libeskind: Jewish Museum Berlin: Between the lines*, Munich, London, 1999

13   See D. Libeskind, *Breaking Ground*, London, 2004. On being a child prodigy: '[I was] an accordian player so good, believe it or not, that I was awarded a prestigious AMERICA-ISRAEL CULTURAL FOUNDATION (AICF) scholarship' (pp. 8–9). On homework: 'After school, I'd finish my homework as I walked home, so that I'd have the rest of the day to practice my technique.' (p. 10)

14   D. Libeskind, quoted in 'Imperial War Museum North; Architects: Daniel Libeskind' in *GA Document*, no. 71, Aug. 2002, p. 26

15   E. Woodman, 'Star Struck', in *Building Design*, no. 1616, 12 Mar. 2004, pp. 12–15

16   A. Styant-Browne, 'Federation Square: A Future About Shatters', in *Architecture Australia*, Nov./Dec. 1997, p. 80

17   Lab, 'Integrating Architecture', in *AD*, no. 123, p. 67

18   A. Styant-Browne, 'Federation Square: A Future About Shatters', in *Architecture Australia*, Nov./Dec. 1997, p. 80

19   C. Jencks, 'A New Heart for Melbourne', *Domus*, Feb. 2003, p. 73

20   Ibid., p. 73

21   A. Brown-May and N. Day, *Federation Square*, Hardie Grant Books, 2003

22   F. Woodman in *Building Design*, 7 Jan. 2005, p. 9

23   Ibid., p. 9

24   See E. Woodman, 'The Sage', *Building Design*, 7 Jan. 2005

25   From a Jean Nouvel lecture in Italy: 'I do not draw as an architect or a designer. Or very rarely so…Whether a project is architecture or design, it develops through "brain storms", exchanges, objective argument and external analysis. I believe in this need for profound analysis.'

26   C. L. Morgan, *Jean Nouvel: The elements of architecture*, London, 1998, p. 25

27   M. Bechthold, 'On Shells and Blobs: Structural Surfaces in the Digital Age' in *Harvard Design Magazine*, Fall 2003/Winter 2004

INFLUENCE (pp. 262–95)

1   S. Sadler, *Archigram: Architecture without architecture*, MIT Press, 2005, p. 167

2   This refers to Le Corbusier's Maison-Domino: a generic column and slab design originally intended for mass-production.

3   T. Ronalds in *Architecture Today*, April 2003, p. 42

4   D. Sudjic, *The Edifice Complex*, London, 2005, p. 298

5   Ibid., p. 298

ACKNOWLEDGMENTS

Many thanks to all the architectural practices who allowed me to publish their drawings.

Individual thanks are also owed to: Bettina Ahrens of GMP Architekten, Sylviane Brossard of Bernard Tschumi Urbanistes Architectes, Caroline Brown and Andrew Griffiths of Airbus, Stefan Camerzind of Camenzind Grafensteiner, Stefania Canta of Renzo Piano Building Workshop, Cindy Cheung of the HACTL Superterminal, Kevin Carrucan of Hassell, Amanda Dahlquist of Studio Daniel Libeskind, Mireia Fornells of EMBT Arquitectes Associats, Katy Harris of Foster and Partners, Christine Gaillard of the Agglo of Rouen, Philip Graus and Russell Lee of Cox Architects, Catherine Langford of Grimshaw Architects, Sandy Lau and Clara Chan of Chek Lap Kok, Catherine Murphy of Terry Farrell, Dominique Price of Will Bruder Architects, Ralf Schirrmann of Messe Frankfurt GmbH, Rikvald Skaaheim of Oslo Gardermoen Airport, Takae Uchibori of Tokyo International Forum. Miki Uono of Toyo Ito and Associates and Carin Whitney of Polshek and Partners as well as Laurie Abbott, Mike Davies, Carmen Marquez, Jenny Stephens and Simon Williams-Gunn of Richard Rogers Partnership.

Thanks also to my friends Andrew and Lorna Camden, Marcus Bleasdale and KB Nøsterud, James Campbell, Pamela Druckerman and Simon Kuper, Ophelia Field and Paul Laikin, Philip and Julie Lewin, Susan Olle, Richard Scott-Wilson and Shona and Mark van Lieshout.

Particular thanks are due to the good and bad cops: Jon and Colette.

FURTHER READING

Alexander, C., and S. Chermayeff, *Community and Privacy*, New York 1963

Allwood, J. (rev. T. Allan and P. Reid), *The Great Exhibitions: 150 years*, London 2001

Amery, C., *Architecture, Industry and Innovation: the early work of Nicholas Grimshaw & Partners*, London, 1995

Andreu, P., 'The Concept of the Kansai International Air Terminal' in *Japan Architect*, no. 15, 1994

Appleyard, B. *Richard Rogers: A biography*, London, 1986

Banham, R., *The Architecture of the Well-tempered Environment* (2nd edn), London, 1984

——, *Theory and Design in the First Machine Age*, London, 1960

——, *Megastructure: Urban futures of the recent past*, London, 1976

Bechthold, M., 'On Shells and Blobs: Structural Surfaces in the Digital Age' in *Harvard Design Magazine*, Fall 2003/Winter 2004

Blaser, W. (ed.), *Norman Foster: Sketch book*, Basel, 1993

Blundell-Jones, P., *C.N.A.R. Alicante*, Stuttgart, 1995

Brown-May, A., and N. Day, *Federation Square*, Hardie Grant Books, 2003

Buchanan, B. S., *Cable-stayed Structures*, Melbourne, 1982

Buchanan, P., 'Kansai' in *Architectural Review* (Special Issue), vol. 196, no. 1173, 1994 Nov.

Burdett, R. (ed.), *Richard Rogers Partnership, Works and Projects*, New York, 1996

Colquhoun, A., *Essays in Architectural Criticism: Modern Architecture and Historical Change*, MIT Press, 1981

——, 'Plateau Beaubourg', in *Architectural Design*, vol. 47, no. 2, 1977

Davies, C., *High Tech Architecture*, London, 1988

——, *The Prefabricated House*, London, 2005

Dunster, D. (ed.), *Arups on Engineering*, Berlin, 1996

Emanuel, M. (ed.), *Contemporary Architects*, St James Press, 1994

Garcetti, G., *Iron: Erecting the Walt Disney Concert Hall*, Glendale, 2002

Giedion, S., *Space, Time and Architecture*, Harvard University Press, 1949

Hardingham, S. (ed.), *Cedric Price: Opera*, Chichester, 2003

Hart, S., 'Buckminster Fuller's Dreams of Spanning Great Distances are being realised in Big Projects: Long-spans amplify the relationship between architects and engineers', *Architectural Record*, May 2002, pp. 267–76

Hawkins, L., 'Sainsbury's Choice', in *Art Monthly*, no. 17, 1978 June. p. 27

Herzog, T. (ed.), *Hall 26 for the Deutsche Messe AG Hannover*, Prestel, 1996

Houlihan, B. (ed.), *Sport and Society: A student introduction*, Sage Publications, 2003

Jansen, H.W. 'Form Follows Function – or does it?', Gary Schwartz Maarssen, 1982

Jencks, C., *The Iconic Building: the power of enigma*, London, 2005

Jenkins, D. (ed.), *On Foster, Foster On*, Prestel, 2000

—— (ed.), *Norman Foster: Works* (vols 1, 2, 4), Munich, London, 2002

Koolhaas, R., *S,M,X,XL*, Rotterdam, 1995

Koshalek, R., et al., *Symphony: Frank Gehry's Walt Disney Concert Hall*, New York, 2003

Kurokawa, K., *Metabolism in Architecture*, London, 1977

Libeskind, D., *Breaking Ground*, London, 2004

Lyall, S., *Remarkable Structures; Engineering Today's Innovative Buildings*, Princeton, 2002

Marcus, G. H., *Functionalist Design: An ongoing history*, Munich, 1995

Marg, V. (ed.), *Expo Halls 8+9 for the Deutsche Messe AG and EXPO 2000 Hanover Gmbh*, Munich, New York, 2000

Moore, R. (ed.), *Structure Space and Skin: The work of Nicholas Grimshaw and Partners*, London, 1993

Morgan, C. L., *Jean Nouvel: The elements of architecture*, London, 1998

Newhouse, V., *Towards a New Museum*, New York, 1998

Nouvel, J., *Architecture and Design 1976–1995: A lecture in Italy*, Milan, 1997

Pawley, M., *Buckminster Fuller*, Grafton, 1992

——, *Norman Foster: A global architecture*, London, 1999

——, *Terminal Architecture*, London, 1998

Payne, M., *Olympic Turnaround: How the Olympic Games stepped back from the brink of extinction to become the world's best known brand – and a multi-billion dollar global franchise*, London, 2005

Pearman, H., *Airports: A century of architecture*, London, 2004

——, *Contemporary World Architecture*, London, 2002

——, *Equilibrium: The work of Nicholas Grimshaw & Partners*, London, 2000

Pevsner, N., *Pioneers of Modern Design* (3rd edn), London, 1974

Powell, K., *Stansted: Norman Foster and the architecture of flight*, London, 1992

——, *Richard Rogers: Team 4, Richard + Su Rogers, Piano + Rogers, Richard Rogers Partnership: Complete works*, vol. 1, London, 1999

——, *Richard Rogers: Richard Rogers Partnership: Complete works*, vol. 2, London, 2001

——, *Richard Rogers: Architecture of the future*, Basel, 2005

Price, C., *Re: CP*, Basel, 2003

Quantrill, M., *The Norman Foster studio: Consistency through diversity*, London, 1999

Ragheb, J. F. (ed.), *Frank Gehry Architect*, Guggenheim Museum, 2001

Renzo Piano Building Workshop, *The Making of Kansai International Airport Terminal*, Kodansha, 1994

Ross, M. F., *Beyond Metabolism: The new Japanese architecture*, New York, 1978

Ruskin, J., *The Seven Lamps of Architecture*, London, 1886

Sadler, S., *Archigram: Architecture without architecture*, MIT Press, 2005

Sasaki, M., 'Structural Design for the Sendai Mediatheque', in R. Witte (ed.), *Case: Toyo Ito Sendai Mediatheque*, Prestel Verlag, 2002

Schneider, B., *Daniel Libeskind: Jewish Museum Berlin: Between the lines*, Munich, London, 1999

Sharp, D. (ed.), *Santiago Calatrava*, London, 1994

Silver, N., *The making of Beaubourg: A building biography of the Centre Pompidou*, Paris, MIT Press, 1994

Steiner, F. H., *French Iron Architecture*, Ann Arbor (Mich.), 1984

Stürzebecher, P., and U. Sigrid, *Architecture for Sport: New Concepts and International Projects for Sport and Leisure*, Wiley-Academy, 2002

Sudjic, D., *Norman Foster, Richard Rogers, James Stirling: New directions in British architecture*, London, 1986

——, *The Architecture of Richard Rogers*, London, 1994

——, *The Edifice Complex: How the rich and powerful shape the world*, Allen Lane, 2005

Tombesi, P., 'Sloppily built or precisely loose? The technology of the curtain and the ideology of Disney Hall', in *Construction*, nos 3/4, 2004

Ward, V., 'A House Divided', *Vanity Fair*, June 2005

Whiteley, N., *Reyner Banham: Historian of the Immediate Future*, MIT Press, 2002

Wilhide, E., *The Millennium Dome*, London, 1999

Wilkinson, C., *Supersheds*, 1996

Woodman, E., 'Star Struck', *Building Design*, no. 1616, 12 Mar. 2004, pp. 12–15

——, 'The Sage', *Building Design*, Jan. 7 2005

Zulaika, J., *Guggenheim Bilbao Museoa: Museums, architecture, and city renewal*, Reno, 2003

Zung, T. K., *Buckminster Fuller: Anthology for the new millennium*, New York, 2001

ORIGINS

POMPIDOU CENTRE
Client: Ministère des Affaires Culturelles, Ministère de l'Education Nationale
Architects: Piano and Rogers (www.rpbw.com) (www.richardrogers.co.uk)
Structural Engineers: Ove Arup and Partners
Services Engineers: Ove Arup and Partners

SAINSBURY CENTRE
Client: University of East Anglia
Architect: Foster Associates (www.fosterandpartners.com)
Structural Engineer: Anthony Hunt Associates,
Services Engineers: Foster and Associates
Cladding Consultant: Tony Pritchard
Main Contractor: RG Carter and Bovis Construction

EXHIBITION

HANOVER HALL 26
Architects: Herzog + Partner (www.herzog-und-partner.de)
Structural Engineers: Schlaich Bergermann
Services Engineers: H.L. Technik

HANOVER HALL 8/9
Client: Deutsche Messe AG, Hannover and Expo 2000 GmbH, Hannover
Architects: von Gerkan, Marg und Partner (www.gmp-architekten.de)
Structural engineers: Schlaich, Bergermann und Partner, Stuttgart

MILLENNIUM DOME
Architects: Richard Rogers Partnership (www.richardrogers.co.uk)
Engineer: Buro Happold

HANOVER HALL 2
Client: Deutsche Messe AG
Architects: Bertram, Bünemann + Partner (project architect Rainer Müller)

MESSEHALLE 3
Architects: Grimshaw Architects (www.grimshaw-architects.com)
Associate Architects: ABB
Structural Engineers: Arup GmbH, Schlaich Bergermann, BGS, Hahn & Bartenbach
Services Engineers: Kühn Bauer & Partners, HL Technik, Dörflinger
Main Contractor: Hochtief/Bilfinger

GRAND PALAIS (LILLE)
Client: Eurolille
Architects: Office for Metropolitan Architecture (OMA) (www.oma.nl)
Associate Architects: FM Delhay-Caille
Structural Engineers: Ove Arup and Partners
Services Engineers: Sodeg Ingénierie
Main Contractor: Dumez-Quillery SNEP

ZENITH (ROUEN)
Client: District of Rouen
Architects: Bernard Tschumi Architects (www.tschumi.com)
Engineers: Technip TPS
General Contractor: Quille

TOKYO INTERNATIONAL FORUM
Architects: Rafael Viñoly Architects (www.rvapc.com)
Associate Architects: Masao Shiina Architects
Structural Engineers: Structural Design Group, Umezawa Structural Design Laboratory, Hanawa Structural Design, Saski Structural Planning Laboratory, Yokoyama Structural Design
Services Engineers: P.T. Morimura and Associates
Main Contractor for glass hall: Katsumara

INDUSTRY

CARGOLIFTER AIRSHIP HANGAR
Client: Cargolifter AG
Architects and Masterplanners: SIAT Architektur + Technik
Structural Engineers: Arup GmbH
Project Management: Hochtief AG

JEAN-LUC LAGARDÈRE BUILDING
Client, architects and engineers: Airbus

HAMBURG MAINTENANCE HANGAR
Architects: von Gerken, Marg und Partners (GMP)
Structural Engineers: Assmann
Client: Hamburg Gesellschaft für Fluganlagen MbH
Project Management: Manfred Stanek, Reinhold Niehoff

NEW YORK TIMES PRINTING WORKS
Architects: Polshek Partnership Architects (www.polshek.com)

IGUS FACTORY
Architects: Nicholas Grimshaw and Partners (www.grimshaw-architects.com)
Structural and services Engineers: Whitby & Bird
Quantity surveyor: Davis Langdon & Everest

HACTL CARGO TERMINAL
Client and project managers: Hong Kong Cargo Terminals Ltd
Lead consultant, engineering design, building project management, supervision and testing: Ove Arup and Partners
Architectural Consultants: Foster and Partners (www.fosterandpartners.com)
FSD Consultants: Loss Prevention Council
Main Building Contractors: Gammon-Paul Y JV
Cargo Handling systems contractors: Mannesmann Demag Fordertechnik, Murata Machinery Ltd.

TRANSPORT

EXPO STATION
Client: Land Transport Authority
Architects: Foster and Partners (www.fosterandpartners.com)
Associate Architects: CPG Consultants Pte Ltd, PWD Consultants Singapore
Structural Engineers: Ove Arup
Services Engineers: Land Transportation Authority, Singapore

OLYMPIC PARK RAILWAY
Architects: Hassell (www.hassell.com.au)

STUTTGART AIRPORT
Architects: Von Gerkan Marg and Partners (GMP) (www.gmp-architekten.de)
Structural engineer: Weidleplan Consulting

HAMBURG AIRPORT
Architects: Von Gerkan Marg and Partners (GMP) (www.gmp-architekten.de)
Structural engineers: ARGE Kockjoy - Schwarz + Dr. Weber

OSLO GARDERMOEN AIRPORT
Client: Oslo Lufthaven AS
Architects: Aviaplan AS with Niels Torp (www.aviaplan.no) (www.ntorp.no)

KANSAI AIRPORT
Architects: Renzo Piano Building Workshop (www.rpbw.com)
Associate Architects: Nikken Sekkei
Structural and services Engineers: Ove Arup and Partners

CHEK LAP KOK AIRPORT
Client: Hong Kong Airport Authority
Design Consultants: The Mott Consortium (Foster and Partners, architects and designers; Mott Connell Ltd, engineering and project management; BAA, airport planning and operational systems) (www.fosterandpartners.com)
Architects: Foster and Partners
Main Contractor: BCJ Joint Venture: Amec International Construction Ltd; China State Construction Engineering Corporation; Kumagai Gumi (HK) Ltd; Balfour Beatty Ltd; Maeda Corporation.

INCHON TRANSPORTATION CENTRE
Architects: Terry Farrell & Partners (www.terryfarrell.co.uk)
Executive Architects: Samoo Architects & Engineers
Structural, Mechanical and Transport Engineers: DMJM
Main Contractors: Samsung/Hyundai/Daewoo jv

BARAJAS AIRPORT (MADRID)
Architects: Richard Rogers Partnership, Estudio Lamela (www.richardrogers.co.uk)
Structural Engineers: Anthony Hunt Associates, OTEP/HCA

Façade Engineers: Arup
Mechanical and Services: TPS, INITEC
Fire Engineers: Warrington Fire Research Consultants
Main Contractors: UTE

SPORT

SYDNEY INTERNATIONAL AQUATIC CENTRE
Client: Civil & Civic for Public Works Department
Architect: Cox Richardson Architects (www.cox.com.au)

SYDNEY SUPERDOME
Client: AbiGroup Contractors Pty Ltd
Architect: Cox Richardson Architects (www.cox.com.au)
Associate Architects: Devine Deflon Yaeger

NATIONAL CENTRE FOR RHYTHMIC GYMNASTICS
  (ALICANTE)
Architects: Enric Miralles and Carme Pinos
  (www.mirallestagliabue.com) (www.cpinos.com)
Structural engineer: BOMA

BUCHHOLZ SPORTS CENTRE
Client: Uster City Council
Architects: Camenzind Gräfensteiner
  (www.camenzindgrafensteiner.com)
Structural Engineers Steelwork: Geilinger Stahlbau
Structural Engineers: Reto Ambass
Cladding Consultant: Mebatech AG
Services Engineers: Planungsgemeinschaft Haustechnik
Electrical Engineers: Schmidiger + Rosasco
Main Contractors: Bereuter AG

ARTS

GUGGENHEIM MUSEUM (BILBAO)
Architects: Frank O Gehry & Associates
  (www.gehrypartners.com)
Associate Architects/ Engineers: IDOM
Structural Engineers: SOM
Services Engineers: Cosentini Associates

WALT DISNEY CONCERT HALL
Client: Los Angeles Philharmonic Association, the Music Centre
  of Los Angeles, Los Angeles County
Architects: Gehry Partners (www.gehrypartners.com)
Accoustics: Nagata Acoustics
Structural Engineers: John A. Martin & Associates
Services Engineers: Cosentini Associates, Levine/Seegel
  Associates
Electrical Engineers: Frederick Russell Brown & Associates
Main Contractors: M.A. Mortenson

IMPERIAL WAR MUSEUM NORTH
Client: Trustees of the Imperial War Museum, London
Architects: Studio Daniel Libeskind (www.daniel-libeskind.com)
Associate Architects: Leach Rhodes Walker
Project Managers: Gardiner and Theobold Management
  Services
Structural Engineers: Arup
Mechanical Engineers: Mott MacDonald
Exhibition Design consultants: Real Studio
Main Contractors: Sir Robert McAlpine

FEDERATION SQUARE
Architects: Lab Architecture Studio
  (www.labarchitecture.com)
Associate Architects: Bates Smart
Structural Engineers: Hyder Consulting
Structural/Façade Engineers: Atelier One with Andrew Watts
Structural Engineers: Bonacci Group
Environmental Engineers: Atelier Ten

SAGE GATESHEAD
Client: Gateshead Council
Architects: Foster and Partners
  (www.fosterandpartners.com)
Structural and Services Engineers: Mott
  MacDonald
Structural Engineers for roof: Buro Happold
Acoustics, Fire and Communications consultants: Arup
Main Contractors: Laing O'Rourke

CULTURAL AND CONFERENCE CENTRE LUCERNE (KKL)
Client: Trägerstiftung Kulture und Kongresszentrum
  Luzern (KKL)
Architects: Architectures Jean Nouvel (www.jeannouvel.com)
Structural Engineers: Electrowatt Engineering AG, Plüss &
  Meyer
Services Engineers: Schudel + Schudel, HVAC
Electrical Engineers: Scherler AG
Accoustic Engineers: Artec
Main Contractor: ARGE Electrowatt Engineering AG/ Göhner
  Merkur AG
Roof contractor: Turschmidt

INFLUENCE

SENDAI MEDIATHEQUE
Client: City of Sendai
Architects: Toyo Ito & Associates (www.toyo-ito.com)
Structural Engineers: Saski Structural Consultants, ES Associates
  Consulting Engineers
Services Engineers: Ohtaki E&M Consulting Office,
  Nishihara Engineering
Main Contractot: Kumagai-Takenaka-Ando-Hasimoto joint
  venture

PHOENIX CENTRAL LIBRARY
Architects: Bruder DWL Architects (www.willbruder.com)
  (www.dwlarchitects.com)
Structural, Mechanical, Electrical and Acoustic Engineer:
  Ove Arup and Partners
Civil Engineers: Hook Engineering
Main Contractor: Sundt Corp

LABAN
Client: Laban
Architects: Herzog & de Meuron
Structural and Services Engineers: Whitby Bird
Main Contractor: Ballast Construction

CITY OF ARTS AND SCIENCES
Architects: Santiago Calatrava (www.calatrava.com)